From Pills to Penicillin

From Pills to Penicillin

The Beecham Story

A Personal Account
by

H. G. Lazell

HEINEMANN : LONDON

William Heinemann Ltd
15 Queen St, Mayfair, London WIX 8BE
LONDON MELBOURNE TORONTO
JOHANNESBURG AUCKLAND

Printed in Great Britain by
Cox & Wyman Ltd,
London, Fakenham and Reading

Contents

1	Early Days in Macleans	1
2	Philip Hill Creates the New Beechams	22
3	The War Years	36
4	Beecham Research Laboratories	45
5	The End of the War – and Afterwards	59
6	We Get Going	70
7	St Helens	77
8	County Perfumery Co. Ltd.	84
9	The Watford Group	90
10	Soft Drinks and Beecham Foods	96
11	Western Hemisphere	114
12	The Discovery	135
13	After Ten Years	151
14	Commercial Development of the New Penicillins	165
15	Europe	171
16	Beecham Inc.	180
17	The End of an Era	189
	Index	203

Photographic Illustrations

Between pages 36 and 37

1   Philip Hill
2   Walter McGeorge
3   Sir Charles Dodds
4   G. J. Wilkins, Sir Ronald Edwards, and Walter McGeorge
5   Sir Ernst Chain
6   The Beecham factory at St Helens
7   The first machine for making Beecham's Pills

Between pages 68 and 69

8   The Duchess of Kent visits the Macleans factory
9   Brockham Park from the air
10   Scientists who pioneered new penicillins
11   Inspecting Penbritin capsules
12   Filling syringes with vaccine
13   The first penicillin plant at Worthing

Between pages 100 and 101

14–16   Beecham's Powders advertised on too broad a front
17   Advertising concentrated on 'colds' alone
18–19   Phensic advertising restyled
20   Ribena strip-cartoon advertisement
21   Adaption for Lucozade

1 *Early Days in Macleans*

In 1938–39 Philip Hill, Chairman of Beechams Pills Ltd. and Chairman and dominant shareholder of Philip Hill & Partners Ltd., bought in quick succession and on behalf of Beechams the businesses of Macleans, Brylcreem, and Eno. In so doing he created what was to become Beecham Group Ltd., which in due course became one of Britain's truly international companies. By this I mean a company which has established a presence in most of the countries of the Western World, this presence taking the form of a company owning assets in, and subject to the laws of, the host country.

I was Secretary and a Director of Macleans Ltd. when it was sold to Beechams in 1938, became Secretary of Beechams soon afterwards, and in 1940 went back to Macleans as Managing Director. Appointed Managing Director and Chief Executive of Beechams in 1951 (and Chairman in 1958), I controlled its destiny for seventeen years until my retirement in 1968.

Sir Ronald Edwards, who succeeded me as Chairman, has pressed me to write the 'History of Beechams' but I am no historian. In any event, I was so personally involved in all that went on that I can only present my own biased story and explain as honestly as possible why particular courses were followed and certain actions taken. Beechams is essentially a 'marketing' company managed since 1951 by marketing men and I have endeavoured to make this story a case history for young men making their way in Beechams or in other businesses of a like nature.

I have chosen to give a brief account of my early years because they help to explain my emotional judgments. We are all influenced by our emotions flowing from our past experiences, particularly in childhood, and most of us use our intellect more to rationalize our decisions than to take them. I was a young man from a happy home with loving parents and grand-parents. However, in business I was on my own, acutely conscious of my lack of formal education and very sensitive to snobbery and nepotism in all their various forms. I never liked being ordered about, was determined to 'get on' and to stand up to the public schoolboys, articled clerks, pharmacists, and chemists with whom I came in contact. I resorted to books and correspondence courses to qualify as an accountant but I always subjected other people's opinions to keen and, no doubt, prejudiced examination and was only too ready to reject them if they did not appeal to me. However, I was reasonably circumspect and kept many of my radical opinions to myself. Many years later, just before I became Managing Director of Beechams, my name came up at some discussions and I was told that Lord Dovercourt said, 'Yes, but he is not one of us'. I suppose that this was so and it must have been clear that I would not conform and 'toe the line'. In those days the university graduate was not much in evidence. Certainly I had little sympathy for a certain type of public schoolboy and even less for those who aped them, but perhaps I reserved the bulk of my spleen for nepotism in all its forms.

I was born in 1903 and soon afterwards was taken to Bombay by my parents where my father took up a position with a firm of wine merchants. My mother brought me back to England towards the end of 1904, as she was having another baby, and during that time my father died of enteric fever, a fatal infection in those days, but now – it should be added – easily dealt with by Beecham's Penbritin.

My first memories are of life with my maternal grand-parents, who kept a lodging house for railwaymen in Camden Town. Mother worked in a millinery shop and our grandmother looked after my brother and me. My grandfather had lost an arm while a shunter on the London, Midland & Scottish Railway and was continued in employment by the railway in some minor capacity at a low wage.

Both my grandfather and my grandmother were the salt of the earth. If I were asked to name the greatest practising Christians that I have known, their names would immediately come to my lips, together with the name of my father-in-law. It seems to me that the practical necessities of those times produced or helped to bring out some wonderful people; we had some grand 'old-timers' in all of our old companies, whose loyalty and concern for the interests of the company was tremendous. They would have been appalled at what goes on in many businesses nowadays. I see no evidence that today's relative affluence has improved the moral fibre of the nation – quite the reverse.

Mother married again in 1909 but we continued to live in a part of my grandparents' house and they gave up taking railwaymen as one-night lodgers. Two more stepbrothers came on the scene, and then the First World War.

My stepfather eventually joined up in the Grenadier Guards under Lord Derby's scheme, and to make some contribution at home, I went to work as an office boy in the department of the Solicitor of Inland Revenue at Somerset House. I was 13½ and was allowed to leave my London County Council school because I passed a 'labour examination'. The Department was not 'established' and when the war ended it was determined that it would become a Civil Service Department and that all permanent staff would become permanent Civil Servants. The temporary clerks, all ex-servicemen who had joined after the war, were to be allowed to sit an examination and, if they passed, were also to be 'established'. After some debate I was allowed to sit the examination and I failed it. This was the greatest bit of luck that could possibly have befallen me; not only did it mean that I had to leave the Civil Service but failing the examination so hurt my pride that I have never failed another thereafter!

I was too proud to go to a Labour Exchange and set about finding a job for myself. In due course I found employment as a book-keeper in a bookmaker's office in Regent Street. I knew nothing about keeping books and the outside auditor who came in to look me over, discovered that I was entering up the cash book the wrong way round! Of course, I was unhappy in my job and set about taking book-keeping lessons at the Working Men's College and passing the examinations of the Royal

3

Society of Arts and the London Chamber of Commerce. This period of my life was a traumatic experience. I had to work on Saturdays and lost my place in the first eleven of the London Polytechnic Cricket Club. In addition, I had met Doris, my future wife, and marriage seemed a long way off. To this day I can still feel the lump in my throat which I got whenever I heard the cinema organ playing 'Parted', a popular ballad of those days.

After eighteen months in the bookmaker's office, where I learnt how simple it was to 'make a book', I got a job as a ledger-keeper with Allen & Hanburys Ltd. of Bethnal Green. It was during my employment with Allen & Hanburys that I took correspondence courses and eventually passed the examinations of the Association of Certified and Corporate Accountants, followed by those of the Chartered Institute of Secretaries. I had been promoted to an accounting job in Allen & Hanburys and Doris and I promptly got married, which we were able to afford because her parents let us have a flat at the top of their house. This was not only financially convenient, but Doris was able to go down to her mother in the evenings whilst I continued my studies.

By 1930 I wanted a change. Allen & Hanburys was living in the past, dominated by pharmacists and no place for a maverick, who had read Adam Smith and had no sympathy with a 'chemists only' policy. Allen & Hanburys were leading supporters of the private retail chemist, who demanded very generous discounts from his suppliers. In those days, Boots were cut-price chemists and Allen & Hanburys used to demand cash with order from them. How times have changed! Now Boots dominate the retail chemist trade and before Edward Heath brought about the abolition of retail price maintenance, led the drive to maintain prices of advertised products.

After many letters to, and one interview with, prospective employers, I got further promotion and ceased my efforts to find another job. Then out of the blue came a letter from Alex C. Maclean asking me to see him at the Strand Palace Hotel. Apparently I had replied to his advertisement some two months previously. He had received many replies and put them all in alphabetical order. Then he set about interviewing a large proportion of the applicants in the same order. In due course he got to the 'L's' and asked me to have dinner with him. We must have 'clicked' because at the end of the dinner he offered me the job of Accountant at Macleans Ltd. at a salary of £350 per annum. I had overstated my age by two years, saying I was 30.

When I gave my notice to Allen & Hanburys everyone thought I was mad. The Sales Manager came to me and asked me if I knew that Macleans were supplying tooth paste to Woolworths. He prophesied that the chemists would break them and that they would be out of business in two years. Allen & Hanburys had been following a 'chemists only' policy in selling their baby foods and I replied that having seen how little benefit they got from this policy I felt sure that Macleans would do well from following the opposite one. Of course, it was its availability in Woolworths that made Macleans Tooth Paste – sales rocketed in both Woolworths *and* the chemists.

Macleans Ltd. was set up in 1919 by Alex C. Maclean, who was born in New Zealand, went to Australia, took part in a gold rush, and then arrived in the United States where he eventually became a salesman for Spirella corsets. He often referred to his experiences in the U.S.A. and alleged that he once saw a lynching. He came to England with a team to set up the Spirella business here, and they were phenomenally successful, building a bigger business than the parent company. All the members of the team had shares in the company and eventually they quarrelled, Maclean marched out and set up his own business manufacturing 'own-name' products for chemists.

In those days the chemist's own-name business was much more important than it is today. All the big pharmaceutical houses sold to the chemist standard preparations to be found in the *British Pharmacopoeia* – such as liquid paraffin, golden eye ointment, and zinc ointment – with that chemist's name, and sometimes his individual brand, printed on the label. This business was extended to cover such products as bay rum, hair oil, bath salts, talcum powders, and the like. It also spread into areas where advertised proprietary brands dominated, such as the tooth paste market. Here the products made up under the chemist's own name were mostly imitations of advertised brands. Old man Maclean had three sons and the eldest, Ashley, ran the factory. He evolved a method of printing tubes in small runs so that the chemist's own brand and name could be printed on them. Hitherto all own-name tooth paste had been sold with a paper label wrapped round the tube and fastened by the clip at the end of the tube. Alex Maclean was convinced that he was going to make a fortune, and he did, but not in the way he had planned.

First of all, the imitation tooth pastes were not very good and some set hard in the tubes. Maclean realized that he had to find a good chemist and in 1923 he noticed an advertisement in the *Pharmaceutical Journal* for a chemist who was looking for a job. He sent for him and in due course along came Walter McGeorge who had graduated as a B.Sc. at Glasgow University in 1922 after some military service in the First World War.

Macleans was at that time installed in Spring Street, Paddington, in what had once been a shop in a terrace of houses. The company occupied the basement, the shop (which was the office), and four floors above. The old man commenced his interview by asking numerous questions; then he called in his son, Ashley, and finally he produced a tin of Zam-Buk Ointment and said, 'Look, can you analyse this?' McGeorge replied that he could if they had any laboratory facilities but, of course, these were non-existent so he went off to the Institute of Chemistry for them. In due course McGeorge reappeared at Spring Street with three tins of Zam-Buk, two genuine and one filled with his own imitation. Alex Maclean called in his son and they smelt them, rubbed them on their hands, and finally Maclean chose one tin as the genuine product. Ashley said he was not sure and left it to his father. McGeorge then turned the tins over and showed that Maclean had chosen his imitation. The old man's reply was, 'Well, you call yourself a Scotsman – why did you go and buy two tins when you could have bought one? Anyway, the job is yours. When can you start?'

Thus Macleans and, ultimately, Beechams, acquired the man who was to provide leadership in the technical field which would enable both companies to compete with the big battalions and ultimately to break into the explosive world of scientific medicine.

Walter McGeorge, or Mac as I shall call him from now on, has become my life-long friend. I certainly would not have achieved what I have without him, nor would Beechams be the company it is today. He possessed that rare ability to explain scientific matters in layman's language. He would listen as well as expound and was universally liked, which was a tremendous asset as the business got bigger.

Alex Maclean was what we would describe today as a marketing man. He was small and very excitable and I carry many memories of his unpredictable ways. In those days of depression and low wages he used to stride around the office waving his arms and declaiming on 'the nimble sixpence', and of course he was talking then of the old pre-decimal kind. He wanted to have a sixpenny size of everything and, indeed, it was the 6d. tube of Macleans Tooth Paste which made the business.

When I joined them in October 1930, Macleans was in the middle of a tremendous upheaval. Around 1927 Alex Maclean had walked into Mac's laboratory, handed him a tube of Wigglesworths Peroxide Tooth Paste and had asked him if he could produce a peroxide tooth paste for Macleans. In due course Mac evolved a pink formula and this was sold to chemists with their own name and address on the tube and carton under the descriptive title 'Peroxide Tooth Paste'. How near it was to the Wigglesworth product I do not know but Wigglesworth never forgave us and in turn copied Macleans Stomach Powder when we put it on the market.

Repeat orders for the tooth paste flowed in and Alex Maclean realized that he had a winner. He promptly put on the market a 'Macleans' Peroxide Tooth Paste coloured white and continued to supply the chemist with the pink formula, under his own name or brand. Both products were sold to the trade at similar prices, with the lowest price at 6s. 6d. a dozen for minimum one gross lots. The Maclean brand had to be advertised and this was possible because of the tremendous savings in packaging costs. In place of tubes and cartons printed in our factory in gross lots, we bought printed tubes and cartons in volume and ran filling lines continuously.

Macleans Peroxide Tooth Paste started to sell well despite some annoyance amongst the chemists at being denied the white product under their own name, but worse was to follow! Alex Maclean was approached by a Mr Parker, the then Woolworths Purchasing Director for toilet products, with a request for a tube of Macleans Peroxide Tooth Paste to sell at 6d. The old man told me Parker had said 'Maclean, if you do this, I will "make" you'. Maclean agreed to produce a tube to sell at 6d. and charged Woolworths 3s. 4d. a dozen in gross lots.

At that time Woolworths were endeavouring to enter the toiletry market but were having difficulty persuading proprietary manufacturers to supply them. The only tooth paste on Woolworths counters was Colgate and when Macleans appeared there was quite an uproar. The chemists threatened to boycott all Macleans products and the Macleans Sales Manager and salesmen were protesting that the company would be ruined. I arrived on the scene in the middle of all this and found Alex Maclean defending his decision against the rest. Major Meade, who had joined the Board after investing £5,000 in the business, led the opposition and confidently expected me, as an 'authority' from Allen & Hanburys, to support him. Instead of that, I argued that Alex Maclean was right and produced figures in support.

By the time I arrived, the sales of the business had rocketed because of Macleans Tooth Paste and the own-name peroxide tooth paste, but no one knew just where all the goods went. There was no sales analysis produced and the only available breakdown of sales was based on orders taken. These figures were wildly out because very large orders were coming in from price cutters whose credit was bad, which were never executed. I did a sales analysis and showed that following our entry into Woolworths, the chemists' sales, in spite of all the protests, had surged ahead. When I took out the figures, Woolworths were responsible for roughly 50 per cent of all sales of Macleans Tooth Paste and the chemists for the rest. But many chemists were slow payers and we had to wait a month or two for our money. Woolworths paid within thirty days of *invoice date* and but for this prompt payment Macleans could not have met its commitments without additional finance. We were over-trading and for eleven months after assuming my duties I had some difficulty with our creditors, some of whom had to wait for their cash.

I liked Alex Maclean; he was excitable and in some ways unpredictable but he had tremendous courage and was a marketing man with no respect for the establishment. Major Meade had no marketing sense and indeed, in my opinion, very little business ability. He was a man with courage and high principles but his social and army background put him at an enormous disadvantage in our sort of business. He had no idea how the masses lived and thought. Meade and the old man were in a constant state of war, which was very embarrassing for all of the executive.

It is interesting to look back on the success of Macleans Tooth Paste in that other world of long ago. Most of the tooth pastes on the market were American – Colgate, Phillips, Koly-nos, Forhans, and Pepsodent (then U.S. owned). They were, in the main, priced high, except for Colgate which I believe was selling at 6*d*. and 1*s*. 3*d*. and was available in Woolworths. All the rest were priced at 1*s*. 6*d*. and above, had no small size, and sales were confined to chemists. Advertising budgets were substantial and I am sure that manufacturers spent 25–35 per cent of their net sales return on advertising. Macleans was priced at 6*d*. and 1*s*. 3*d*. and in the early days 20 per cent of one month's sales was appropriated to be spent in the succeed-ing month or months! At no time did Macleans invest any money in its tooth paste – it had not got any! Chemists got very substantial discounts on branded proprietary goods, sometimes as high as 40 per cent. They marked up their own-name goods by enormous percentages; buying Peroxide tooth paste at 6½*d*. a tube they would offer it for sale at 1*s*. 6*d*., 1*s*. 9*d*. or even 2*s*. Macleans Peroxide had to be sold at 1*s*. 3*d*. and so the chemist who bought on best terms got 8½*d*. for handing it over the counter and Macleans got 6½*d*. for manufacturing, delivering,

advertising, and carrying the credit to the chemist for upwards of three months! No wonder I developed strong views on
the evils of privilege and believed in Adam Smith's dictum that
all business associations eventually became a conspiracy against
the public. I felt that the chemist was a gross example.

In my view, Macleans Tooth Paste succeeded because, first
of all, it was a product with a unique flavour which really did
clean teeth, and then it hit the market at the right time. Tooth
pastes were selling at higher prices than they should. The inter-
wars slump was in full swing and prices were falling. Money
was short and the unit price of many products, certainly toilet
preparations for the masses, was vital. It was the period during
which Woolworths built its business on the principle of selling
nothing above the price of 6d. The nimble sixpence, as Alex
Maclean put it. Dentifrices were sold mainly through chemists
who demanded wide margins and did not favour low unit
prices. Our competitors therefore chose to maintain high prices
and spend more on advertising. Alex Maclean chose to follow
Colgates and sell at the low price. He was terribly handicapped
at the start because his own-name business forced him to give
a large discount to the chemists, but this had an advantage in
that it gave them a good profit on the sale of Macleans and
persuaded many of them to refrain from any overt attack on
the company's products. The chemists took notice of Woolworths, and themselves stocked the 6d. size. Very quickly we
were selling four 6d. tubes for every 1s. 3d. tube.

Macleans Tooth Paste gave me my first lesson in 'marketing',
a term not coined in those days. When he was ready to advertise the tooth paste, Alex Maclean walked into the offices of
Bensons, the biggest advertising agents in the country, and demanded to see a director. He was passed over to Norman
Moore, a young associate director who became Account Director for Macleans and who remained closely associated with the
company right up to the time when he retired from the Chairmanship of Bensons. Norman Moore was a wise and diplo-
matic adviser. His company produced very fine advertising for
Macleans over many years and Norman's pressure to continue
merely to offer Macleans for cleaner teeth in the face of ever-

stronger claims by competitors, taught me a lesson I have never forgotten. Time and again I have found that the best advertising is that which makes a simple single claim based on the truth.

The success of Macleans Tooth Paste altered everything at Macleans. Profits had been fluctuating and low until own-name Peroxide tooth paste was launched. Meade had put his £5,000 in the company in return for a Debenture with an option to convert into Ordinary Shares. As soon as profits started to rise he went along to a Board Meeting with a formal notice to convert his Debenture. This was before my time but I was told that before he could do so Maclean moved that the Debenture be paid off. Of course, there was an unholy row at the meeting and Maclean withdrew his motion and allowed Meade to convert. I was also told that Maclean was right in law and need not have given way.

When I joined the company it had a factory and offices at Park Royal, just outside London. They were temporary wooden buildings put up during the First World War and subsequently converted into a trading estate. Everything was pretty spartan and I had quite a shock on my first day when I viewed the offices. Alex Maclean had an office near the front door and Meade one beside him. Macauley, the Sales Manager, had the only other private office and beside these were two large rooms, one a Sales Office and one the Accounts! My desk – a small typist-type one – was at one end of the Accounts Department and my symbol of office was a plastic pen holder and pen. There was not room for many people and this encouraged us to avoid the 'British disease' of overmanning at least in the offices.

Stomach Powder

Some time around 1929 there had appeared a paper in the *Lancet* or the *British Medical Journal* (I forget which) by Professor Hugh Maclean of St Thomas's Hospital (no relation of Alex) on the intensive alkaline treatment of stomach ulcers. This got press notice and chemists even sent in orders to Macleans Ltd. for some of the powder. Eventually Alex Maclean became interested, consulted Mac, and took him to see Professor Hugh Maclean. The meeting was very pleasant and cheerful and the two members of the clan Maclean got on well together. Alex said that he would like to put the Professor's powder on the market and enquired how Hugh stood in relation to the product. The Professor replied that there were no patents and nothing to stop Alex going ahead, but that he, of course, as a scientist could not be associated with the venture in any way. He did, however, recommend a particular mixture (there were several) as being cheaper but Mac rejected this advice and chose another one which contained more bismuth.

By this time we had been joined by a new Sales Manager, F. C. Hewett. He was a protégé of Meade and soon provided additional cause for quarrels with the old man. Hewett felt very insecure. He was a 'medicine man' and naturally searched for a medicine to which he could attach himself and win credit for its success. He found it in Maclean Brand Stomach Powder. His advocacy was so enthusiastic that the old man in his inimitable fashion started to argue against him and challenged Hewett to prove his words. Maybe Alex considered this the best way to achieve success and, as he was certainly not a 'medicine man', it was no doubt a good thing for the company that Hewett took over the marketing.

Hewett engaged a friend of his named Eric Field as advertising agent and they commenced a 'reader' campaign which I considered misleading. The 'reader' advertisement in those days was a single column of varying length (three or six inches usually) in the news section under a headline which looked exactly like a news headline. In the case of Macleans the headline usually had some reference to 'hospitals' and the body of the advertisement held out Maclean Brand Stomach Powder as the powder used in hospitals for the treatment of stomach and duodenal ulcers.

The product went like a bomb and again we were able to appropriate a percentage of the previous month's sales to advertising, without having to invest any money. It clearly was a very good formula for indigestion, but I wish that we had not been so unscrupulous. Certainly it created an opening for the many imitations to establish a position in the market, as they went one better and made reference on their package to Dr Hugh Maclean and St Thomas's Hospital. As a result, poor Hugh Maclean was the victim of a lot of slander suggesting that he was drawing royalties on his formulae and the use of his name. The Maclean advertising did not really change until Beechams purchased us and Hewett departed.

At this time the proprietary medicine business was under attack largely generated by the Pharmaceutical Society, the National Pharmaceutical Union, and their journals. Of course, there was plenty of misleading advertising to attack, although I did not believe that the motives of the chemists were altogether altruistic. They were continuing their age-long fight to get the sale of medicine restricted to chemists and to see that the proprietary brands were decimated so that they could return to the days when most medicines were 'made up' by a pharmacist. These were the days before the wonder drugs, when very few specific remedies were available. The doctor relied heavily on his 'bedside manner' and undoubtedly one who was able to gain the confidence and faith of his patient achieved more 'cures' and made a reputation. So with the proprietary medicines – advertising was of paramount importance and, if it were believable, could work wonders.

Many different types of people resorted to proprietary medicines but particularly those who suffered, or imagined they suffered, from a complaint that the doctors were unable to cure or were indifferent to. Rheumatism was a case in point and there were many remedies extravagantly advertised, used extensively by sufferers, who often went the rounds from one to another, usually finding some relief real or imaginary. The proprietary medicine formulae were not usually fraudulent – they had to be harmless and mild in effect and relied heavily on aspirin. There was nearly always a psychological content either in the flavour, appearance, or action if and when placed in water. Hewett once said to me that an advertised medicine must have some immediate perceivable effect – if it only made people break wind.

I looked askance at this business for a long while and certainly considered that a great many people active in it were frauds. But I gradually came to the view that what was needed was the elimination of the frauds. There exists throughout the world a great demand for 'health'. Very few people will accept the fact that their complaint is hopeless and that no cure or even relief is available. They will continue to look for something that brings them relief and if the doctor does not give them sympathy and hope they will resort to the advertised medicines. There was ample evidence from the perfectly genuine testimonials that flooded into Macleans that stomach powder and, later, Fynnon Salt were relieving human misery; no doubt imagination played a part but who can deny that a lot depends on our imagination? Even today the 'image' that is created around a product affects our enjoyment of it, whether it be a Savile Row suit, a Rolls-Royce car, a pot of face cream or an aspirin tablet. To return to our sufferer from rheumatism, he or she needed something to take, in which he or she believed. My mother-in-law took Fynnon Salt during the last twenty years of her life and was convinced that it kept her rheumatism at bay. So does my sister-in-law today and our cook, now retired. Their faith in it was and is absolute and for them – and I believe for tens of thousands more – it works.

I cannot go deeply into the history of the proprietary medicine business. Suffice to say that there grew up an association of manufacturers called the Proprietary Association, supported by all the large proprietary medicine companies, which 'cleaned up' the business and set a pattern for other industry associations that followed. The Association has earned great respect from Government, and other trade associations, and it is also listened to with respect abroad, particularly in Europe and the U.S.A.

There came a day, some time in 1933, when stomach powder sales passed those of tooth paste and Hewett went up to the old man, his face alight with triumph, and a piece of paper in his shaking hand containing the figures. Alex Maclean was furious and waving his hands over his head declared that the day would come when tooth paste sales would be double those of stomach powder. As usual, he was right! The day came when tooth paste sales were ten times those of stomach powder in this country and over fifty times worldwide.

We were now in pretty good financial shape and the Park Royal factory was clearly inadequate for our needs. Meade began looking for another site. Allnatts, the builders, came along and sold us a plot of land on the Great West Road, with a condition attached that they should build the factory. This was a pretty unsatisfactory arrangement, although the site was first-class. Fancy plans were produced which looked fine from the outside but gave uneconomic space inside. Mac did his best to improve the layout and bore the brunt of all this argument and all the trouble resulting from the cost-plus agreement. We never did get a logical building but the factory was not so bad; it was the offices which were a mess.

Fynnon Salt

In 1935 our travellers began to report on a product called Fynnon Salt which was selling well in the chemist shops, apparently because of a story circulating widely that it had been recommended by Lord Horder, the King's Physician. The story took various forms and, indeed, sometimes the name of Lord Dawson of Penn was used, but the commonest tale went as follows:

> Two cars came into collision on a country road. They both stopped and with great difficulty an old lady was helped out of one, bent over and obviously in pain. The occupant of the other car came up and showed great concern, asking if the lady had been injured. On being told that she was suffering from rheumatism, he said, 'Allow me to recommend a remedy' and producing his visiting card wrote 'Fynnon Salt' on the back. The card was that of Lord Horder.

How this story started I do not know. We made a sustained effort to find out and our travellers were instructed to make enquiries during their calls on chemists. On one occasion a traveller reported that a chemist had a drawer full of cards, some of which were Lord Horder's, and he was certain that one of these had Fynnon Salt written on the back. He was sent back at once to get it but reported that the contents of

15

the drawer had been thrown away! I cannot believe that Lord Horder ever recommended Fynnon Salt, but neither can I explain how such a rumour could circulate so widely that the demand for Fynnon completely outstripped supply.

Fynnon Salt was evolved by Evan Jones, a Welsh chemist with a shop in Caerphilly. He had developed a substantial local business that had spread to other parts of England. When he died he left the Fynnon Salt business to his wife and two daughters and the chemist shop to a son. The mother and younger daughter moved to Warrington in Lancashire to live with the married daughter, whose husband ran the Fynnon Salt business from the home, using a garage to store the tins and fill them from time to time with crystalline sodium sulphate purchased from the company British Drug Houses. Orders came in and were filled but no advertising was done. The total annual sales were small and profits were regarded as pin money. Then came the rumour, orders flooded in, and they were quite unable to meet them.

When I called on the family with Mac they showed me the grand piano open, and full of orders, many with cheques and money orders attached. It was a fantastic sight. The Maclean Board were frightened of buying the whole of the Fynnon business and I therefore suggested that we bought 60 per cent, leaving 40 per cent in the hands of the family. This was quickly settled and the family agreed to sell 60 per cent of the business for £10,000. Later on we had to pay £40,000 for the balance, a substantial penalty for our lack of courage.

We formed Fynnon Ltd., issuing the necessary shares and completing the legal formalities, whilst we took charge of the backlog of orders and commenced filling at Brentford. It quickly transpired that British Drug Houses could not supply us with the quantity of sodium sulphate required. This was a special needle crystal which was formed after a liquid concentrate had been run into shallow tanks. The needles grew down from the surface and were then filtered off. British Drug Houses were not prepared to increase their deliveries beyond the capacity of their existing tanks, which took up a lot of floor space, unless we gave them a two-year contract. The price of the salt was high and Mac and his Consulting Engineer, Ernst Koch, were convinced that we could produce the crystals in quantity at a fraction of the cost. We therefore took the decision to take all British Drug Houses could give us from their existing plant and to institute a crash programme to develop our own manufacturing process and plant.

The full burden of all this fell on the shoulders of Mac and Ernst Koch. Koch was a German Jew who had left his homeland soon after Hitler came to power and, by the time we knew him, had obtained British naturalization. He was an extremely able chemical engineer. From 1934 until his untimely death in 1948 he served Mac faithfully and was largely responsible for a growing standard of technical excellence, first in Macleans and then in Beechams. He had a big hand in setting up Beecham Research.

A bigger company would never have achieved the results we did so quickly. There would have been too many meetings, capital appropriations to be approved, and reports to the Board. Mac only had to get verbal approval of a global sum of expenditure and go ahead. During the short period in which the process was developed and the plant erected, neither he nor Koch had much spare time or home life. Certainly I often looked in late at night to find them still at work with their engineers.

Their new Fynnon Salt process rested on utilizing drum dryers and refrigeration. The process was unique and was patented by Macleans Ltd. Because of the urgency, all the plant was second-hand, searched out and purchased by Koch. Moreover, the plant was erected in the open at the same time as the building to house it was going up. Long before the building was completed, Fynnon Salt was coming off the plant, which was operating within a few weeks of the purchase of the business. We caught up with the backlog of orders within two months. The staff, of course, had collected substantial overtime but Mac and Koch only got an allowance for one suit and two pairs of shoes each, eaten into by the sodium sulphate. Later on the sodium sulphate also ate away at the foundations of the building – a much more expensive operation!

17

Once Fynnon Salt was coming off our own plant in adequate volume, we ceased to order from British Drug Houses and commenced advertising. Hewett again used Eric Field and once more they resorted to 'reader' copy. Sales rocketed and we now had three highly successful proprietaries.

Perhaps I should pause here and try to conjure up a picture of this small successful business which must have been typical of many up and down the country.

In those days the executive did not expect to get rewards other than his salary. Income tax was relatively low and one could live well and *save* on one's salary. We bought our own cars and cheerfully used them on the company's business, without recompense. We used to entertain on behalf of the company, again without making any charge. Indeed, as Directors, we would have considered it *infra dig.* to do so. What a difference today – and all because of a stupidly excessive tax charge on the higher incomes!

There was a very definite division between office and factory conditions of employment. Office workers were paid weekly and received two weeks' holiday in a year. The factory workers got one week, and whilst the men were paid and employed by the week, the girls were liable to be sent home at short notice when stocks were high and packaging lines were shut down. In effect they were sacked and told they could report back on a given date for re-employment. These girls were employed on the moving-band packaging tables where most of the work was done by hand or with hand-operated machines. They were controlled by a very tough woman who would not hesitate to smack their hands when they were not operating efficiently. Girls usually came straight from school at 14 years of age earning 14s. per week, rising by 1s. a year, until they reached the maximum of 18s. at 18. After this, unless they were promoted to forewomen, they were sacked. Automatic packaging machinery was available from the U.S.A. and Sweden but it was not considered worthwhile to install it whilst wages were so low. Of course the last war altered all this.

There were many other differences in the treatment of office and factory staff in the early days in such matters as hours of work, sick pay, and pension plans. They were gradually equalized as the company became more successful. I cannot remember who had most influence on improving staff conditions before the war, but Major Meade was sympathic. When Lord Amery became Chairman of the Board he took a great interest in working conditions and persuaded the Directors to grant a family allowance of 5s. for every child of an employee after the first two. We then discovered that we had an Irishman working in the factory earning £3 per week with fourteen children back in Ireland. His pay was doubled and I hope he sent the money home.

Money bought a lot in those days and people's wants were simpler. Most of our people seemed happy in their work and the social barriers between office and factory staff did not seem great or rigid. We bought and equipped a fine sports ground near the factory and our football and cricket teams came from all over the business. The social club ran numerous functions including dances where again people seemed to mix in well. Major Meade was keen on squash rackets and eventually we built a squash court right in the factory. It was at one end adjacent to the stores and to reach it during daytime from the office one had to walk down the main factory corridor past all the filling tables. Often in the morning Meade would poke his head round my door to enquire if I were busy and would I like a game of squash? We used to change into singlets and shorts in our lavatory (which had a shower) and then walk past all the little girls working away packing tooth paste, Meade completely oblivious and myself doing my best to appear unconcerned! Our squash team was quite good and we had some great times playing other teams in the evening. I am sorry to say that here we made no effort to recruit factory staff, who never appeared interested.

Business in those days at Macleans was quite lighthearted and we managed to see the funny side of everything – even the Meade/Maclean quarrels. There were some fine characters in the factory, some of whom had been Welsh miners. To find work, they had walked from Wales to London along the Great West Road and had enquired at the factories on the way in.

Mac employed a number of them and we never had more loyal workers. They accompanied us into Beechams and moved in various directions then, some to Brockham Park and others to Worthing. All made a fine contribution to the morale of the business and I hope that they also feel that their life has been rewarding.

Our First Public Issue

Meade was particularly anxious to 'cash in' some of his fortune in Macleans and had been arguing strongly for a public issue. 'Mossy' Myers, of the stockbroking firm of Myers & Co., was consulted and in 1935 we issued 750,000 Preference Shares on the market. To facilitate this the Rt. Hon. L. C. M. S. Amery, P.C., M.P. (later Lord Amery) was appointed Chairman of the Board and Alex Maclean resigned. He was getting old and had become tired of fighting Meade. The Board then consisted of Amery, Chairman; Meade and Ashley Maclean, Joint Managing Directors; and Guy Maclean, the old man's second son, who had not long joined the business. Hewett and I joined the Board in 1936, he assuming the title Sales Director and I retaining my office as Secretary and assuming the title of Director and Secretary. The issue was a success: £100,000 was used in the business and £650,000 paid out to the shareholders. In spite of my steady support for Alex Maclean, Meade had shown me the utmost friendliness. He was responsible for persuading the Ordinary shareholders (mostly family, but one substantial 'outsider') to sell 2,000 shares each to Hewett and myself and 1,000 to Mac, the shareholders providing them *pro rata* to their holdings. We had not got the money to pay for these shares but loans were arranged from the Bank. This made all three of us 'capitalists'. When Macleans sold out to Beechams my shares were worth £20,000 and I was well able to repay the Bank the £4,000 borrowed.

We were now a substantial company with three well-known proprietary products. For the year ended 31 March 1937 our profits before tax were £266,000. I represented the Company on the Committee of the Proprietary Association and also on the Dentifrice Manufacturers Committee of the London

Chamber of Commerce. Here I came in contact with the managers of subsidiaries of the great U.S. international businesses, such as Colgate, Sterling Drug, and American Home Products. This made me realize how vulnerable British business was to U.S. competition and how important it was to improve our efficiency and, above all, to develop our research.

2 *Philip Hill Creates the New Beechams*

Hitler had now risen to power in Germany and Meade, who had friends in politics and also in quarters interested in Germany, started to predict war. Both Maclean's and Meade's families were worried about death duties and the position of the business should either Maclean or Meade die. Meade was particularly concerned at what would happen to the company in the event of Maclean's death, and he wanted to offer a substantial block of the Ordinary Shares to the public. The market, however, had been shaken by some unfortunate issues. In the proprietary field in particular, shares in Eno had been put on the market, profits had fallen, and the shares were standing much below the issue price.

Then in 1937 we were introduced by our lawyer, Mr F. A. S. Gwatkin, to Mr Diebold of Sterling Drug Inc. of the U.S.A., who wanted to buy us. Sterling Drug was one of the largest proprietary companies in the U.S.A. They sold all over the world such products as Bayer Aspirin, Phillips Milk of Magnesia and Tooth Paste, Andrews Liver Salt, and California Syrup of Figs.

Meade wanted to sell; Maclean was indifferent and Ashley, as usual, followed Meade. I was very keen to sell and did all I could to encourage the deal. I had seen the U.S. proprietary companies operating in England and recognized that they were more 'professional' than the British. I wanted to get inside an American business so as to find out how it ticked. We gave Diebold all our figures and I had long talks with him about the business. Then came the bombshell; he received a cable from Weiss, the Chairman of Sterling Drug, saying that in view of the imminence of war in Europe the Board had decided that the company could not undertake any further commitments there.

This only increased Meade's urge to sell. He had been quite insulting to Mr Philip Hill when he had made an approach, and had told him that on no account would Macleans sell to Beechams Pills Ltd. None of us wanted this to happen because in those days, Beechams had no reputation in the trade and was certainly not out of the top drawer in the City.

However, in the summer of 1938 'Mossy' Myers appeared again. He persuaded Meade and Ashley Maclean to see Philip Hill and before long we were in serious negotiation. It did not take long for a deal to be worked out. In those days, Philip Hill's favourite method was to acquire a business for cash, finding the bulk of the money by issuing Preference Shares. In our case, he formed Beecham Maclean Holdings Ltd. in July 1938 as a subsidiary of Beechams Pills Ltd. and offered £1½ million of 5 per cent Preference Shares of that company to provide most of the purchase price of £2,221,000. In those days he was able to buy profits at about five to seven times earnings and the money cost him about 8 per cent. The difference between the cost of servicing the Preference Shares and the profits of the company, of course, accrued to the benefit of the Beechams Pills Ordinary shareholders. It was mainly by this method – used to acquire a succession of businesses such as Yeast-Vite, Dinnefords, Amami, Phyllosan, etc. – that Philip Hill brought about the early rise in the value of Beechams Ordinary Shares on the Stock Exchange. From 1931 to 1939 they rose in value by 76 per cent. It should be remembered that this covered a period in which there was certainly no inflation.

Even during the negotiations I had my first clash with Bernard Hobrow. He was a Chartered Accountant, the Secretary and, in effect, Headquarters Administrator of Beechams Pills Ltd. Macleans had a profit sharing scheme which appropriated a small percentage of profits over a base figure to a fund and shared it out amongst senior executives according to points allocated. It was proposed to pay this off in cash and I undertook to persuade the executives to accept, provided that I was satisfied with the terms. Hobrow made a number of proposals designed to reduce the amount of cash compensation, which I thought unfair, and as a result we had an argument which became quite a clash of personalities. Philip Hill then intervened and withdrew the offending proposals.

By this time I was even less enamoured of Beechams Pills Ltd. It had been provided that all the Macleans Directors should be given five-year contracts but when this was brought up at the meeting, I said that I, personally, would prefer not to have a contract – 'They may not like me and I may not like them!'. Meade got very agitated and when we were alone appealed to me to stand together with the other Directors. I never liked contracts and, as soon as I became Managing Director, service contracts became exceptional in Beecham Group, only being used for chemists to protect the companies' know-how.

It was obvious to all of us that the seat of power in Beechams was at King Street where Philip Hill sat in the offices of Philip Hill & Partners Ltd. He was a burly man, not very tall, but to me he always loomed larger than life. There was an aura of power about him and he sat at the end of a long room which one had to traverse to get to his desk. It was quite an ordeal to walk the length of that room under his direct gaze.

There can be no doubt that Beecham Group was created by Philip Hill. He started life as an estate agent and he possessed an instinctive judgment of the value of a business. He was, of course, a financier first and last. On one occasion I took a man to see him whose business I wanted to buy. The prospective seller brought along his bank manager who knew Philip Hill and they got talking about Reginald McKenna who had just died. Philip Hill expressed surprise at the smallness of Mc-Kenna's estate, and our prospective seller, who was a little put out at being excluded from the conversation, said, 'Oh, but Mr Hill, there are rewards in life other than money'. Hill looked at him for a moment and said, 'What are they?' At another time he said to me 'The important thing is to buy the right business – it is easy to buy management!'

I cannot agree with his last opinion but he certainly bought the right businesses when in quick succession he acquired

Macleans Ltd., Eno Proprietaries Ltd., and County Perfumery Co. Ltd. (Brylcreem). I had heard that there had been concern amongst his Directors that he was paying too much for Macleans. Some of them certainly thought that he was paying a ridiculously high price for Brylcreem and Hobrow told me that they were going to vote against the purchase at the Board Meeting. When the time came, Philip Hill put his resolution to the meeting, looked round the table and everyone held up his hand! Sometime afterwards he said to me, 'Lazell, if I had listened to these b.... I would never have bought a business'. He was a man of immense integrity and prided himself that his word was his bond. He never expected to be asked to confirm anything in writing and so far as I am concerned, possessed the two qualities I most admire – integrity and courage.

Lucozade

During our negotiations with Beechams in 1938, Hewett came to me with John Gibson, one of our travellers, who told me about a Mr Hunter, the owner of a chemist business named W. Owen & Son, of Newcastle. Newcastle was a substantial medical centre and Owen & Son, being near the Newcastle Infirmary, filled many prescriptions from the consulting physicians of that area. At that time, jaundice was prevalent and the doctors were prescribing glucose – 'mixed with fruit juices to taste'. People were coming back to Hunter's shop, complaining that their invalid could not keep the glucose down, no matter what they mixed with it. Then Hunter's own daughter was taken ill with the complaint. Hunter had equipment to carbonate water in the basement of his shop and he conceived the idea of producing a carbonated drink containing as much glucose as he could get in, and flavoured with a mixture of lemon and orange oils. In due course the drink was produced, tried successfully on his daughter and some other customers, and after testing and further experimentation put on the market as Lucozade.

Our traveller, John Gibson, told us that the business in Lucozade had become too big for Hunter to handle and that he was prepared to sell. I looked at the product and concluded that the cost of freight would make it impossible to sell nationally from the Maclean factory. We were not in the soft-drink business and had no bottling plants spread around. However, Gibson would not be put off and came to see us again with the figures. We looked at these and discovered that if we could achieve nationally the sales already being made in the Newcastle area, we would have a turnover of over £1,000,000 per annum! I went off to Newcastle post-haste with Mac and Koch, our Consulting Engineer.

Hunter was a Scot who had served through the First World War in the Medical Corps. He and Mac hit it off immediately but clearly he had reservations about Koch and myself. We became good friends afterwards and he told me that he had gone home to his wife and said, 'Thank God there was a Scotsman to balance two Jews'. Koch, of course, was a Jew and I had a streaming head cold and probably looked like one. Indeed, when I once attended a Sader in Israel and donned the little round cap, Isaac Wolfson said to me, 'Leslie, you only need to be circumcized to be one of us'.

We spent all day inspecting Hunter's plant and in negotiating a deal, subject to our Board's approval. Finally we agreed a selling price of £90,000 with a provision for an additional capital payment related to sales in excess of £100,000 per annum during the first two years. We were to form a separate company and Hunter was to join the Board at a salary.

By this time the purchase of Macleans by Beechams was being completed. I had hardly met Stanley Holmes, the Managing Director of Beechams, and so I telephoned Philip Hill and said that I wanted to get approval to purchase Lucozade. He called at the Macleans offices on the Great West Road on his way up to London from his home at Sunningdale the following Monday morning, listened to what I had to say, looked at the figures, and said, 'Buy it'. I got the agreement signed and sealed as soon as possible, Mac and Koch got busy setting up a bottling line at our Great West Road factory, and we were in business. Then Stanley Holmes came along and gently reminded me that I should have spoken to him. He said that I had greatly embarrassed him because he had already refused to let Henry Gregory, the Managing Director of the Veno Drug Co. Ltd., another Beecham subsidiary, buy the business. Gregory ever afterwards had a bottle of Lucozade on his desk when Holmes visited him. Years later I learnt that Sterling Drug, the U.S. company who decided not to buy Macleans, also refused to allow their British subsidiary, Scott & Turner Ltd., makers of Andrews Liver Salt (also in New-castle), to purchase Lucozade. What they missed! For a time after the war Lucozade was providing about one-third of the U.K. profits of Beecham Group. Today it has been over-shadowed by the worldwide business of Brylcreem and Tooth Paste and, of course, by the antibiotics, but its importance to Beechams in the decade 1951–61 cannot be exaggerated.

Not long after Macleans was acquired by Beechams I was asked to move to 68 Pall Mall as Secretary of Beechams Pills Ltd. At the same time, Hobrow was appointed Assistant Managing Director. Beechams had a very large number of subsidia-ries, but no attempt was made to rationalize or consolidate the business acquired. They were left to carry on under managers who were, in the main, underpaid and uncontrolled. Sir Stanley Holmes was Managing Director and he visited the companies at regular intervals to discuss the business and to express his wishes, if any. Headquarters was an accounting office. The whole accounting system of Beechams was first-class, much superior to Macleans. Hobrow had joined Beechams as Secretary in 1930. He was a fine accountant, particularly in the sphere of investigations, and the Beecham subsidiary ac-counts were designed to disclose all indirect and capital expenditure in a whole series of schedules attached to the year-end accounts. No manager could indulge himself without seeing his extravagance in black and white at the end of the year!

Once a month we held a whole series of Board Meetings starting with the subsidiaries and finishing with Beechams Pills Ltd., as the parent company was still called. The meetings were almost wholly financial in content, and it was unusual for a small subsidiary's meeting to take more than five minutes. Directors of the various subsidiary companies (there were 'outside' directors on some Boards) waited in an adjoining room and on one occasion I was very embarrassed to find that a meeting had been concluded before an outside director had joined it! The whole set-up was crying out for rationalization. Very few Beecham directors knew anything about the proprietary business and the men who actually ran the subsidiaries were not represented on the main Board and certainly had no time or, for that matter, inclination, to parade their problems at their own Board Meetings. Hobrow had been appointed Assistant Managing Director and with the two of us at Headquarters there was nothing much for me to do other than run the monthly circus, except when another acquisition was underway. Fortunately for me, and for Beechams, Philip Hill made two more major acquisitions before war broke out, when he acquired Eno Proprietaries Ltd. in 1938 and County Perfumery Co. Ltd. (Brylcreem) in July 1939.

J. C. Eno (Eno Proprietaries became the holding company) was a very old business, curiously enough, like Lucozade, originating in Newcastle, which was also the home of its principal competitor in the U.K. – Andrews Liver Salt. Also like Lucozade, Eno's had been evolved by a local chemist as, incidentally, were may of the early proprietary medicines.

Seamen using the East Coast ports were heavy users of Eno's and by taking it with them on their voyages brought about an overseas demand that helped to build the business worldwide. This had been steadily developed and by 1938 there were Eno companies in Canada, Australia, South Africa, many countries in South America, and in the U.S.A. By far the greater proportion of the company's sales were overseas.

Brylcreem, on the other hand, was a relatively new product that had achieved rapid growth in the U.K. It was a unique water-in-oil emulsion which broke down instantly when applied to the hair, moistened it, and kept it from drying out. Previous hair preparations had been based on alcohol, which dried out the hair and scalp, or plain oil which was messy, or they contained gum which set the hair like a board and caused dandruff. As a result of its superiority and the fine marketing of N. F. Fabricius and his advertising agent George Royds, Brylcreem

28

made very rapid progress and at the time of its acquisition dominated the U.K. market. It had made some progress abroad but the foreign business was very patchy and all done by means of agency or joint marketing agreements.

George Royds played an important part in Beechams' affairs before the war and during the immediate post-war years. He advertised most of the company's proprietary medicines and built the Amami business with his slogan 'Friday night is Amami night'. He was concerned in the successful marketing of Brylcreem and in its acquisition by Beechams, and after the war provided the advertising which built the Lucozade sales. In those days advertising rested very much on 'hunch'; consumer research was unheard of and test-marketing not nearly so prevalent. George had an instinct for good advertising. He could correctly foresee the way Mrs Smith or Miss Brown or Joe Bloggs would react to particular stimuli and I considered him a great advertising man. He was the only person I met who forecast the defeat of Winston Churchill in the 1945 Election. There were many who claimed to have so predicted but I never heard them until afterwards!

With the acquisition of Macleans, Eno, and Brylcreem, Philip Hill swamped the old proprietary medicines and laid the foundations for Beecham Group as we know it today. These three companies provided the products for our overseas development with Eno's 'Fruit Salt', Brylcreem, and Macleans Tooth Paste. Furthermore, from Eno Proprietaries and, to some extent, Macleans, Beechams acquired the overseas companies through which its worldwide business was developed.

In the year to March 1938 Beechams' sales were £1,862,000, practically all proprietary medicines, and profits £598,000. For the year ended March 1941 (the first full year which included all three acquisitions) sales were £6,231,000 (including £1,470,000 of toiletry products) and profits £1,062,000.

It is impossible to predict what would have happened to Beechams if the war had not intervened. Philip Hill had fashioned a powerful group, and if he could have procured good management I am sure he would, by means of further acquisitions, have quickly built a great international company. He made it clear that he had this in mind when he acquired Eno and immediately made contact with Gordon Dunbar, the Eno Director responsible for their overseas business. I was not a party to the discussions between them, but I am sure that Philip Hill was questioning Dunbar to find out what companies he should go for to enable Beechams to rival the great American international proprietary businesses.

However, *management* was already emerging as the primary Beecham problem. I cannot illustrate this better than by quoting below in full a report to the Board by Stanley Holmes. Several Committees were proposed but only in regard to overseas business was any attempt made to concentrate management, and this was largely on the initiative of Philip Hill.

MEMORANDUM FROM THE MANAGING DIRECTOR OF BEECHAMS PILLS LIMITED

The addition to the Beecham Group of such important businesses as those of "Maclean" and "Eno" makes it desirable that consideration should be given to the following matters.

1. That a number of men whose ability has been stamped with the hall-mark of success have now joined the Beecham Group.
2. That their Companies may, either at home or abroad, have adopted selling or advertising methods which might advantageously be adopted by other Companies in the Group.
3. That, on the other hand, methods successfully pursued by the Beecham Group might be found to be suitable for adoption by the new members; and
4. That there may be, as a result of the recent additions ways by which economies may be effected.

Before dealing with these matters, it may be desirable to state that the policy of the Beecham Group has been to operate its various businesses as separate entities with their own factories, office staffs and travellers, with the exception of some small acquisitions which have been taken over by larger companies.

The following are short details of the businesses of the present Beecham Group.

Beechams Pills Ltd.
Factory and Office Staff at St. Helens, Lancashire.
Manufactures and distributes:—

> Beechams Pills
> Beechams Powders
> Beechams Lung Syrup
> Lactopeptine

has two sets of travellers, one for chemists and one for small wholesalers and hucksters. The latter set, in addition to Beecham Products, seeks orders for Amami and Sherley goods and Yeast-Vite screws.

Veno Drug Co. Ltd.
Factory and Office Staff at Chester Road, Manchester.
Manufactures and distributes:—

> Dr. Cassells Tablets
> Venos Lightning Cough Cure
> Germolene
> Phensic

has two sets of travellers, one for chemists and one for small wholesalers and hucksters. The latter set, in addition to the above products, seeks orders for Holloway Pills screws and Holloways Ointment in 3*d*. tins.

Irving's Yeast-Vite Ltd.
Iron Jelloid Co. Ltd.
Cicfa Co. Ltd.
Factory and Office Staff at Watford.
Manufactures and distributes:—

> Yeast-Vite
> Iron Jelloids
> Cicfa

has one set of travellers who call on Chemists only.

Phosferine (Ashton & Parsons) Ltd.
Moving this month to new factory at Watford with office staff.
Manufactures and distributes:—

Phosferine (liquid and tablets)
Ashton & Parsons Baby Powders

has one set of travellers calling on Chemists only.

Natural Chemicals Ltd. (Phyllosan)
Factory and Office staff at Clipstone Street, W.1.

Phyllosan Tablets are imported from Berne, Switzerland and are packed and distributed here.

One set of travellers, who also carry Dinneford's Magnesia and Holloways Pills and Ointment.

Dinneford & Co. Ltd.
Holloways Pills Ltd.
Factory and Office staff at Clipstone Street, W.1.
Manufactures and distributes:—

Dinneford's Magnesia

Packs and distributes:

Holloways Pills (made by Beechams)
Holloways Ointment (made by Veno's)

Prichard & Constance (Mfg) Ltd.
Factory and Office staff at High Holborn, W.C.2.
Manufactures and distributes:—

Amami Products

Has set of travellers.

A. F. Sherley & Co. Ltd.
Factory and Office Staff at Marshalsea Road.
Manufactures and distributes:—

Sherley Products (some of which are made by Beechams and Veno's)

Has set of travellers.

Macleans Limited
Factory and Office Staff at Great West Road, Brentford, Middlesex.
Manufactures and distributes:—
(inter alia)

Macleans Stomach Powder
Macleans Peroxide Tooth Paste
Fynnon Salts

Has set of travellers.

Eno's Proprietaries Ltd.
Manufactures:—

Eno's Fruit Salt at Pomeroy Street, S.E.14.
Thermogene at Haywards Heath

and has Office Staff at Piccadilly, W.1.
Has set of travellers.

The basis of the recommendations made in this memorandum is that Committees, composed of Directors and Managers, should be appointed with terms of reference dealing respectively with important matters with which the Group has to consider, that such Committees should meet at least monthly and should report their recommendations at such intervals to the Board of Beechams Pills Ltd.

It is suggested that Home Trade and Export Trade should be regarded as separate problems and should be considered accordingly.

It is recommended that three Committees should be appointed, viz:—

1. Home Trade Advertising.
2. Home Trade Sales.
3. Export Trade.

1. Home Trade Advertising. This Committee would be dealing with the most important matter of all. It would give consideration to the copy used for the various products, the agents employed, the prices paid for space and other cogent matters.
2. Home Trade Sales. This Committee would deal with the contact with Chemists and other retailers and the extent of the duties of the various sets of travellers. It would consider the "pack" of all products, and generally would deal with all matters which concerned sales stimulation.
3. Export Trade. The Committee appointed for this purpose would deal with the export trade in all its aspects.

The above-mentioned Committees would be of a permanent nature, only varied in personnel from time to time by decision of the Board of Beechams Pills Ltd.

It might be considered advisable that a temporary "ad hoc" Committee should forthwith be appointed to consider whether any entity of the Group which at the moment is operating by itself should be amalgamated with or absorbed by another member of the Group, or even without amalgamation or absorption should transfer its operations to the factory of another member.

Such are the recommendations which I submit for consideration. It is necessary that I should add that a colleague has submitted alternative suggestions which should equally be considered.

As regards Home Trade, he suggests that a Marketing Company should be formed to undertake the whole of the selling of all the products of the Beecham Group (except Sherleys and Prichard & Constance). This Marketing Company would employ such travellers as might be necessary: all orders would be sent to the various Factories; the goods would be despatched by them but the invoicing would be done by the Marketing Company and the collection of Accounts would be undertaken by it. The expenses of the Marketing Company would be distributed over each Company upon an equitable basis according to turnover. This Marketing Company should have a Sales Committee which would consider monthly:—

Travellers Reports
Analysed Sales figures
New lines, and
Results of new types of advertising.

It should also have an Advertising and Development Committee to:—

View all new copy
Consider new forms of advertising
Fix advertising expenditure for each Company
See that competitive advertising does not appear in the same newspaper on the same day.

The Marketing Company might also purchase all raw materials for the various Companies, including Stationery, cartons, showcards, etc.

As regards Export Business, my colleague suggests that an Export Company should be formed on the same lines as his proposed Marketing Company, except that the Export Company will deal with Export business only.

Signed J. STANLEY HOLMES
10th October 1938

35

3 *The War Years*

On the initiative of Philip Hill, Beecham Export Corporation Ltd. was incorporated in July 1939 with Gordon Dunbar, the Eno Export Director as Managing Director, just in time to take over responsibility for most of the company's overseas subsidiaries as the Second World War broke out. Nothing else was done to rationalize the Group's affairs during the war, except in response to acts of war, such as the bombing of the J. C. Eno factory in the East End of London.

Early in 1940 Meade and Ashley Maclean sent in a report recommending evacuation of the Maclean offices to Farley Court, Meade's house near Reading. The Maclean factory on the Great West Road nestled amongst some of Britain's prime factory targets and they were fearful of the effect of bombing on the Maclean accounting system consisting of Powers-Samas punched cards. These were the only record of the company's debtors. Philip Hill asked for my opinion and I expressed strong disapproval, pointing out that it would set a terrible example to the factory staff. I said that I was sure we could put the Powers-Samas machine and its cards in a properly ventilated underground room which could be made bomb-proof, and Ernst Koch was immediately instructed to get one built.

Soon afterwards Philip Hill called me over and said he wanted me to go back to Macleans as Managing Director. He said that he knew that Meade wanted leave of absence during the war to take a job in the British Red Cross, and he asked me if I had any suggestions as to what would persuade Ashley Maclean to vacate his position. I knew that Ashley's wife was pressing him to take his children to Canada and I therefore suggested that he should be offered a job with Harold F. Ritchie Ltd., the Canadian subsidiary of Eno Proprietaries Ltd. The offer was made, Ashley accepted, and on 12 June 1940

1. Philip Hill.

2. The author and Walter McGeorge (*right*).

3. Sir Charles Dodds.

4. Three generations of Chairmen talking to Walter McGeorge: (*from left*) G. J. Wilkins, the author, Mac, and Sir Ronald Edwards.

5. Sir Ernst Chain.

6. At St. Helens the original Beecham building, complete with clock tower (*right*), was built in 1880. The modern additions date from after the last war.

7. The first machine used for making Beecham's Pills.

Meade was given leave of absence; Ashley resigned and I was appointed Managing Director of Macleans Ltd. and, soon afterwards, a Director of Beechams Pills Ltd. I have often wondered whether I was right to put temptation in Ashley's way.

So far as I was concerned, the war years provided a concentrated education in management and labour relations. They developed and solidified my basic beliefs and when I eventually took charge of Beechams, I was greatly helped by the principles and methods developed at Macleans during the war.

The circumstances of war applied a magnifying glass to everything and forced quick decisions. Raw materials were short or non-existent, often rationed, of varying quality, and obtainable irregularly. Formulae therefore had to be changed frequently, with inadequate time for testing. This called for a strong group of scientists, but these were also wanted for other jobs more directly concerned with the war. We had a comparatively low priority, in spite of the fact that cosmetics and toilet articles, particularly tooth paste, were considered essential to the morale of the population and in spite of the fact that we became the largest producers of anti-gas ointment.

I had my first brush with the Civil Service over this anti-gas ointment and learnt early in life what an immovable elephant it is. We received our first contract with a precise formula and process. Mac came to me and said that he was sure that this formula would set hard in the tube within a matter of months. He went along to the Department with his suggested alternative formula which he predicted would remain stable for a long period. He was snubbed and got absolutely nowhere, and we were instructed to follow out the directions. We did, and sure enough in two months' time we had millions of tubes of anti-gas ointment as hard as rock.

Tooth paste gave us our greatest problem. It was a very delicately balanced formula containing 40 per cent of glycerine. Soon after I arrived on the scene, I got a call from the Controller of Soaps and Fats who had been seconded to the Ministry of Food by Unilever. He asked me to lunch to talk about glycerine and I went with Mac, whilst he had with him Dr Clark, the chief Unilever scientist. After a very good lunch we were judged in fit condition to withstand the body blow. Tooth paste manufacturers were to get no more glycerine, but were to be allocated sugar to make an equivalent volume of sugar syrup. They realized that this would hit Macleans hardest and had concluded that we could not produce the Maclean formula, or anything like it. Dr Clark had come along to offer us any help he could give us from Unilever and said he had several formulae which we could use during the war under some other brand. I thanked him and we came away.

During the Meade/Ashley Maclean regime and in the absence of any leadership from above, an unofficial committee of Mac, the Buyer, and the Sales Manager had considered a great many problems that would arise in the event of war. They realized that they would lose their glycerine supplies very quickly and Mac had pointed out that the only substitute would be sugar syrup. Unlike Dr Clark, Mac was sure that he could make Macleans Tooth Paste with sugar syrup and, indeed, had made some up. The Buyer was confident that sugar would also be in short supply and that as all allocations of essential raw materials were made on the basis of consumption in the year preceding the war, it was concluded that no good purpose would be served by carrying out much work on sugar syrup. As a result, no formulae were put on long-term storage tests.

When we got back to the factory we were faced with a major crisis. Mac immediately got to work on the alternative sugar syrup formulae. He warned me that none of them were likely to remain stable for the length of time that the original did (it remained in perfect condition for more than two years) but as a shortage of tooth paste was already developing, we did not believe that long shelf life was necessary.

Glycerine soon ran out and we had to decide whether to go ahead with the best sugar syrup alternative, or wait for three months to find out how it stood up in the tube on the shelf. We decided to go ahead, shipped the goods, and laid down shelf tests at the same time. For a while everything went well and then came the shock.

Some time before the war, as a result of one of Meade's

drives for lower costs, we had purchased tubes from a new supplier. We had not then any system of scientific testing of packaging materials and, indeed, Mac had no authority over the packaging, which was under Ashley Maclean. Subsequently, it was discovered that the tubes were not pure tin, but tin-coated lead. However, the original formula stood up in them, although in use there was more black mess at the nozzle due to abrasion. As a result of all this Mac and his collaborators invented the idea of the white plastic nozzle (the first of its kind) which enabled us to revert to the use of tin-coated lead tubes and save a lot of money. We had to be careful and subjected the tubes to continuous scrutiny to determine that an effective coating of tin covered the inside. No one posed the question whether the new sugar syrup formula would stand up in tin-coated lead tubes, and it did not. There was a lot of water in this formula and as soon as temperatures got above a certain point, molecules of lead exposed where the white nozzle was clenched into the tube migrated to join with molecules of sulphur from the vulcanized rubber of the wad in the cap. This formed lead sulphide and the first squeeze of what was a white tooth paste came out of the tube black!

Complaints started to come in and we had immediately to commence a major withdrawal from the market. It cost us nearly £100,000 by the time we had finished and as we had then to use pure tin tubes our costs went up astronomically.

I was astonished at the ease with which we regained our share of the market. Of course, there was a general shortage and that helped enormously. We had also got the bulk of the stock back from the wholesalers and retailers with great speed. However, I think that the sugar syrup formula also helped, because it was sweeter and when we returned to the glycerine formula after the war, we took care to make it sweeter.

Everything emphasized the need for more scientific control in Macleans. It was impossible to build up our laboratories with British scientists but, fortunately for us, there were quite a few high-class scientists who were refugees and who were not trusted to work in jobs with high security risks. We employed some of these men and they gave us very good service. Because he was originally a refugee from Germany, and in spite of the fact that he was a naturalized Britisher, Koch himself did not get conscripted for vital war work. He had one brother in Germany who was a Nazi and another who was a Communist! It was our good fortune to have him, as he was invaluable to Macleans and to other companies in the Group.

Immediately the war started prices of raw materials and packaging began to rise. Stanley Holmes was most anxious to hold down prices. He felt that it was our duty to do so and he authorized all companies to lay down large stocks. This policy was no doubt desirable up to a point, but stocks deteriorate and great care had to be taken to rotate them properly. We had a lot of trouble in Macleans and if I had my time over again I would not have laid up as much stock as we did.

I completely disagreed with the policy of holding down prices and pressed the point that I wanted to maintain advertising and pursue quality wherever possible. Holmes let me have my way in Macleans but other companies followed his desires and Brylcreem finished the war with a wholly inadequate margin for advertising and profit. Amami, which at that time dominated the shampoo market, was ruined by slavishly pursuing this policy. Its products were all sold at low unit prices to the masses. Miss Samuels, who managed the business, scoured the country to buy cheaper raw materials (much to Mac's horror) and reduced the quality of her packaging materials. The result was that the brand steadily lost ground and eventually had to be merged into County Laboratories (Brylcreem).

It was my view then, and now for that matter, that the great increase in purchasing power suddenly released by the very substantial rise in wages and salaries, ought to be soaked up, in part at least, by higher prices, particularly of luxuries and semi-luxuries. To hold prices down at the expense of quality (which was what happened in Amami) was not even what the public wanted. I was intensely interested to notice that our factory girls immediately resorted to higher priced cosmetic and toiletry articles and even started to buy Jaeger slacks to wear in the factory in place of those bought at the local shop in the High Street. The 6d. packs lost their appeal and larger sizes became popular. After the war many attempts were made to get back to small sizes but in the main these failed, and in the proprietary business we were never again to be dominated by price.

The war continued to create conditions of crisis and provided all of us who remained managing the business with invaluable training. Staff were transferred to the Armed Services or to 'war work'. Most of our young girls left for the Services or munition factories and we eventually existed on the help of part-time married women. One shift came in the morning, finishing with lunch in the canteen, and the other shift started with lunch in the canteen, and then went to work. The key to getting good staff was the quality of the food in the canteen! The married women 'took over' and needed very different handling from the young girls or even the men. They were very good indeed and were soon making suggestions for improving their operations. The last bastion to fall to them was the Tablet Department. Tableting was then considered an art, not a science. The foremen were a law unto themselves and had their own secret tricks. I remember that at Allen & Hanburys the scientists attempted to gain control of the Tablet Department and laid down 'standards'. These the foreman contemptuously followed and soon complaints were coming in from the public that tablets were passing right through them without disintegrating. When the Maclean Tablet Department staff were reduced to much below normal, we diffidently suggested to the foreman that he take on some selected married women. He was at first implacably opposed, but he could not make any alternative suggestion and eventually gave way. The women moved in and within a few months were pushing the foreman around and arguing about his little secret tricks. We were then able to discover precisely how our tablets were made and get down an exact record. That was how, thanks to the wartime married women, we managed to reduce tableting to a science.

Lucozade became a major concern during the war. Glucose was rationed and we were not able to acquire more than we had purchased in the year preceding the outbreak of hostilities. Lucozade was in great demand in sickness and we received a growing volume of letters, especially from doctors, appealing for supplies. It was of particular use in cases of serious illness where the patient could not take solid food and it was rationed to chemists, who were requested to supply it only in known cases of sickness. We considered many ways of increasing supplies and finally a very highly qualified Austrian refugee chemist on our staff came forward with an assertion that we could make glucose from horse-chestnuts. He demonstrated this in the laboratory to Mac's satisfaction but, of course, there were many imponderables that should ideally have dictated a systematic approach. However, the horse-chestnut season was nearly upon us and if we let it pass we should lose a year. We decided to take the risk. The Ministry of Health was contacted and gave its blessing. Women's Institutes, Boy Scouts, and Girl Guides up and down the country agreed to collect horse-chestnuts for a fee of 2s. 6d. a sack, dispatched to us carriage forward.

It was, of course, impossible to buy new plant and Koch got busy acquiring what we required at second-hand. In spite of all his efforts we had to accept some plant not entirely satisfactory and in particular we could not obtain all the stainless steel or glass-lined vessels required. This ultimately proved our undoing.

The collecting programme was a great success and soon hundreds of tons of horse-chestnuts started to flood into the Brentford sidings of the railway. The manager of the yard came to us in a great panic complaining that we were impeding the war effort. He said that his sidings were choked with wagons filled with chestnuts and that the whole of the Southern Railway was in disarray because of our purchases. A fleet of lorries was hired and soon a great mound of sacks of chestnuts started to grow on the spare land inside the factory site. Underneath was the underground room housing our punched-card accounting equipment and we felt all the safer at night when the bombs were falling and we held our Management Meetings there!

Meanwhile, the plant had been erected and Mac and his collaborators started to process the chestnuts. The first problem was the presence of saponin, an ingredient in those days widely used in foam fire extinguishers. Foam came out of every joint in the plant and it took many weeks to evolve a process which got the last particle out. Then we were faced with iron contamination. The process was an acid one and inevitably removed iron from those vessels not glass-lined or made of stainless steel. Finally, Mac came to me and said that unless and until they could get stainless steel plant, and also solve the problem of a mysterious trace of phosphates, they were unable to produce uncontaminated glucose. This was a blow; the mound of chestnuts had grown to noble proportions and weighed over 1,000 tons. Fortunately, as most boys know, chestnuts get hard with age and it appeared that even the rats had ceased to gnaw at them. So there they remained until the war ended and we faced the winter of 1947 and the serious coal shortage of that year. Industry was rationed and Macleans was put in a category that would have involved us in a total shutdown of about a month's duration. Then Mac came to me and pointed out that horse-chestnuts had about half the calorific value of coal. He thought that if we mixed coal and horse-chestnuts in equal proportions we could run our boilers adequately. So it turned out; we were able to keep the factory open through the winter and all our costs of collection and storage (which had not been written off in the books) were more than covered by the saving of coal. I began to feel that I had been born under a lucky star!

The war caused some of the Group's smaller businesses to take the first steps towards merging. For instance, Dinnefords had small premises in the West End, which became untenable because of the bombing, and Sprott, the Manager, brought the business to Macleans where we manufactured for him. When he died after the war Macleans took the whole business over.

N. F. Fabricius had plenty of problems in County Laboratories. Brylcreem needed large quantities of light oil which they were unable to obtain regularly. They also required substantial quantities of beeswax, only to be obtained from Africa or South

America, and this did not present itself either in sufficient quantity or quality. The Brylcreem formula was altered substantially, to reduce the oil and beeswax content and much was learnt which was of value after the war. Had it not been for this experience our claim in the U.S.A. that Brylcreem was 'not messy – not sticky' would hardly have been true.

There is not much else I can say about the war years. Most managements were isolated, and my only contacts were with those businesses we were called on to help or with those nearby like County. My strong recommendation to increase our research effort came entirely from our Maclean experience.

4 Beecham Research Laboratories

Towards the end of his life Philip Hill became interested in scientific medicine through his friendship with Professor E. C. Dodds (later Sir Charles Dodds) who was the inventor of stilboestrol and in charge of the Courtauld Institute. Then Philip Hill was put in touch with a Swiss named Henry Spahlinger who had studied medicine, but had not qualified. Spahlinger claimed to be able to cure tuberculosis and a great many other complaints. He was a great showman and had persuaded the Government of Northern Ireland to run a test of his system for the prevention of tuberculosis in cattle. Of course, he made great play with this when selling himself to his prospective patients. His basic line of patter was health, and he held himself out as a living example of what could be achieved. He had black hair (which I suspect was dyed), was very active, and claimed to be a great age.

Being unqualified, Spahlinger was unable to accept fees. Nevertheless he was attending a number of big names in industry and politics (Socialist as well as Tory) and in one case within my knowledge the person he treated had tuberculosis. Spahlinger also had a wonderful 'pitch' on improving male powers, to which on one occasion he subjected me. He was lecturing me on health and went on to say that a perfectly healthy man of my age should have sex several times a day. When I observed that this would become rather boring, he replied that it need not take place with the same woman and that he could take care of that!

Spahlinger's basic plan was to put people under an obligation to him and then in due course to ask for a favour, or offer something for sale or his services as a consultant. He was offering to sell Beechams secret formulae for potential new medicines and I had to advise Philip Hill against buying them. Mac

45

assured me that they were formulae little different from those to be found in the *British Pharmacopoeia* or Martindales. Furthermore, Mac and I had visited Spahlinger's laboratories: they were populated with voluptuous women, solemnly operating equipment that Mac could see was out of order and not in a condition to provide answers. I ought to make it clear that to someone ignorant of science, or medicine, Spahlinger was impressive and that but for his attempt to suborn me with sex and but for Mac's technical advice, I might well have come under his spell.

By 1942 Philip Hill was a sick man under more or less continuous medical care and there developed a battle between Sir Charles Dodds and Spahlinger for the ear of Philip Hill and Beechams. There are in existence minutes of two Special Committees of Directors, chaired by Philip Hill, to discuss the possibility of setting up a Research Board. I give in full the minutes of the first one, held on 1 April 1942:

> The Committee considered the advisability of setting up a central Research Board and Laboratory for the Beecham Group companies. It was agreed unanimously that it was essential to look ahead now and that the future of patent medicine businesses lay, to a large extent, in the development of ethical or semi-ethical specialities. It was pointed out that ethical products already had a very large market in America, Germany and France, and it was considered that the trend in this country would also be in this direction. The following broad principles were generally agreed:—
>
> (1) The Research Board should not be composed of chemists already employed by Group companies as they were already fully engaged in maintaining the standards of present-day products.
> (2) Special consideration should be given to biological and bacteriological research.
> (3) The primary objects of such a laboratory should be:—
>
>   a. To keep in touch with scientific research all over the world, and advise individual companies of any discoveries that might be of interest to them.

   b. To maintain the standards of present formulae.
   c. To explore fresh fields with the idea of producing remedies that would be constructive in addition to merely satisfying public demand.
(4) The services of two or three of the leading scientists should be employed to advise on both the setting up and running of a research laboratory, and it was suggested that the advice of Dr Drummond, Dr Plimmer and Professor Dodds should be sought in this matter.

   After further discussion Mr Spahlinger was requested to prepare a memorandum on the line in which he felt this research should be directed, and it was agreed that the Managing Director should see Professor Dodds, and that Mr Lazell and Mr Dunbar should consult Dr Drummond and Dr Plimmer.

Spahlinger attended this meeting, but not Sir Charles. He refused to attend any meeting which included Spahlinger. Then on 22 April 1942 we have the following minute:

   The Managing Director read to the Committee a letter he had received from Professor Dodds with reference to the establishment of a Medical Research Board by Beechams Pills Limited. After discussion it was Resolved that Mr Holmes should communicate further with Professor Dodds as to whether he would be able to help in this research and which would be the best way of approaching the problem.

This is all we have in the records. Sir Charles won his battle with Spahlinger who ceased to have any influence on Philip Hill. However, Spahlinger made contact with Hobrow and later on with Buckley, as a result of which Mac and I had a lot of trouble fending him off after the death of Philip Hill.

By 1943 I had become an enthusiast for research. It is difficult to remember all the reasons but certainly Spahlinger had nothing to do with it and I had not had much contact with Sir Charles Dodds at that time. I do not believe that I was particularly interested in the so-called 'ethical' medicines.

47

Indeed, for a long time my interest was centred on finding some outstanding drug for sale to the public. The continuous work on tooth paste and the many laboratory attempts to make glucose economically had stirred my mind but perhaps the two greatest influences on me were Mac and U.S. competition. Mac was a born scientist and was never so happy as when in the lab going over the work and suggesting various courses of action. He was also speculating on how to improve our products or how to improve on competition.

Then there was U.S. competition. Although I had never visited that country, I had become fascinated with the U.S.A. and what I had read and heard of the harsh competitive climate there. I had witnessed and experienced U.S. competition in Great Britain from such great companies as Procter & Gamble, American Home Products, Sterling Drug, and Colgate-Palmolive. I knew and, in some cases, was friendly with the managers of the British branches. It was apparent to me that after the war we were going to be hard put to compete with them effectively, and I felt certain that we would not do so unless we built up first-class research laboratories. I therefore put a report to the Board which commenced as follows:

Beechams Pills Limited control a group of companies largely concerned with the sale of proprietary medicines. The net profits of the Group are in excess of a million pounds per annum and to date very little money has been allocated to research. Only one Company in the Group possess what can properly be called Research Laboratories.

During the past two years at Macleans Limited we have extended our laboratories and are employing scientists who can properly be called Research Workers. I have recently been given permission to add a Biological Laboratory and am in the process of making arrangements to this end.

Recent events both in this country and overseas lead me to the conclusion, however, that what has been done and what we are proposing to do is inadequate and will not meet the needs of the post-war situation. In my submission the

Beecham Board should be prepared to allocate at least £50,000 per annum to research and that these sums should be allocated in the knowledge that results will not accrue for some considerable period. Provided the money is properly spent, I am sure we shall eventually reap a rich reward and in the meantime the mere fact that these laboratories are in existence may be of great help to us in the immediate post-war period.

The full report is reprinted at the end of this chapter.

I must have had discussions with Philip Hill prior to presenting the report and in accepting it I am sure he must have been influenced by the advice of Sir Charles.

As will be seen from the full report, I envisaged that we would reward our scientists by means of royalties but this we were never able to do. It turned out to be impossible to determine the relative contributions made to any piece of work and any attempt to do so would have stoked up the fires of jealousy, I imagine never far from the surface in any research institute. Then there were the consultants, and the need to keep them fully informed. Due to the influence of Sir Charles Dodds we relied heavily and, I believe, uniquely, on outside consultants and it was imperative that they knew all that was going on. It was difficult enough to persuade some of our scientists to make full disclosure of their work, anyway, and if royalties had also been at stake we would have had great trouble. Again, all income suffered high taxation, but a higher salary was more valuable than a royalty because the 'top hat' non-contributory pension depended on rate of salary. So the scientist's contributions were recognized by salary increases and promotion to Boards. Whether we did enough is open to question. Certainly our scientists in course of time moved from being our lowest paid category of staff to amongst our highest, but they never seemed to be so interested in money as, say, the marketing people, and I think they suffered in consequence.

The report came before a Beecham Board, chaired by Philip Hill, which approved it in principle. However, we were in the middle of the war and it was decided that until it was possible

49

to establish the laboratories in a separate location, they should remain with Macleans and be built up there as much as possible.

Fortunately, the Finance Act 1944 revolutionized the tax treatment of research expenditure. Prior to that, such expenditure was disallowed as an expense of the business on some ludicrous reasoning. The 1944 Act provided that all research expenditure not of a capital nature be allowed as a charge in the year in which it had occurred, and that expenditure of a capital nature be allowed as a charge spread equally over a period of five years.

The word 'research' was then and is now used very loosely. I certainly had in mind mainly what we in Beechams now call 'product research'. This term covers the improvement of formulae, either in effectiveness, elegance, flavour or perfume, and also utilization of new compounds coming on to the market and evolving elegant formulations from them. Last but not least, I thought that it was imperative to watch competitive moves and to match them if they proved interesting.

In the early days we made a great many mistakes and, in particular, that of attempting too much. Anyone only had to have an idea (and I was one of the principal culprits) and we would have another project. We could not carry on like that for very long before it became obvious that we were on the wrong tack.

We decided that our final home for research should be a country house. Mac and Koch started a search for a house south of London. They took me to several likely ones, and I drove Philip Hill out to one in which we were interested. Then they saw Brockham Park and from that time on there was no doubt where we wanted to be. Brockham Park at that time consisted of the main house, a dower house, ten cottages, stabling, an indoor riding school, and 150 acres of land, including 30 acres of parkland. It was occupied by what was called a 'Pre-OCTU', which was a place to which men from the ranks were sent by the Army to be tested to see if they were officer material. In January 1945 we bought everything – subject to Army occupation – for £25,000. Subsequently we sold off most of the land (other than 30 acres of parkland), the dower house, and some of the cottages and realized practically the whole of our purchase price. I suppose that today the whole estate would be worth somewhere in the region of a million pounds and it could be said that we were wrong to sell anything, but then, as I shall recount in the next chapter, research was under attack at Board level and I felt it was better to support a policy that kept down expenses and also to cut out activities which could have given rise to further attack.

Beecham Research Laboratories Ltd. had been formed in March 1945. Mac was appointed Managing Director and joined the Board of Beecham Group Ltd. in November 1945. Prior to this he went to the U.S.A. He actually left in convoy and was in America when Germany capitulated. His main purpose was to investigate the manufacture of penicillin and to ascertain whether we could make an agreement with one of the U.S. manufacturers for manufacturing know-how. This came about because during the war I was approached by Dr Alexander McGregor through the Macleans lawyer, Mr F. A. S. Gwatkin. Dr McGregor was a dental surgeon dealing with airmen whose mouths had been badly injured in air combat. He had developed a soft gelatine pastille impregnated with penicillin which he used before and after operations, to combat infection in the mouth. These pastilles were very successful and we manufactured a lot for the Royal Air Force hospitals.

I began to get interested in penicillin and speculated that in due course it must be made available for general sale – at least for external application. This idea that penicillin could one day be bought over the counter had great influence on my mind and was the principal reason for my continued interest in it. It has not come about and I am sure that Mac and the Beecham scientists agree that it should only be supplied on doctor's prescription. However, I am an unrepentant maverick and am still prepared to argue, for instance, that ampicillin, Beechams' broad-spectrum new penicillin, could with advantage be made available for advertisement and sale to the general public, subject to adequate safeguards as to what is said in the advertisements and on the package. Had it not been for my wrong-headedness about penicillin I doubt very much whether we would ever have entered the field of microbiological research.

Mac made the rounds of the pharmaceutical companies in the U.S.A. but could find nobody prepared to supply us with know-how and came back to report that we could not go it alone.

Then in mid-1946 the Army vacated Brockham Park and Mac, with Ernst Koch and his team, set about converting the place into a research laboratory. This was not easy at a time when everything was in short supply and when one could hardly move without having to get a licence from someone. I must confess that we took many short cuts and, in addition, relied heavily on Koch's ability to find second-hand materials. And so by 1947 we were at last established at Brockham, a name pregnant in Beecham history.

The complete report to which I referred earlier follows:

Proposals for the Formation of Beecham Research Laboratories Limited
[dated 12 May 1943]

Beechams Pills Limited control a group of companies largely concerned with the sale of proprietary medicines. The net profits of the Group are in excess of a million pounds per annum and to date very little money has been allocated to research. Only one Company in the Group possesses what can properly be called Research Laboratories.

During the past two years at Macleans Limited we have extended our laboratories and are employing scientists who can properly be called Research Workers. I have recently been given permission to add a Biological Laboratory and am in the process of making arrangements to this end.

Recent events both in this country and overseas lead me to the conclusion, however, that what has been done and what we are proposing to do is inadequate and will not meet the

needs of the post-war situation. In my submission the Beecham
Board should be prepared to allocate at least £50,000 per
annum to research and that these sums should be allocated in
the knowledge that results will not accrue for some considerable period. Provided the money is properly spent,
I am sure we shall eventually reap a rich reward and in the
meantime the mere fact that these laboratories are in existence
may be of great help to us in the immediate post-war period.

In any attack on the patent medicine industry and on the
Beecham Group in particular we could, if such Research Laboratories were in operation, point to the fact that the Group's
preparations were backed by modern research laboratories,
staffed by eminent scientists. Even if an attack does not develop,
the knowledge that the Beecham Group is backed by modern
research might help considerably to destroy any prejudice in
official minds and might persuade sectional interests that they
would be unwise to launch an attack on us.

Assuming that the Board approves this policy in principle
then we have to consider how best to put it into effect and in
this connection I suggest that the following principles should
always be borne in mind:—

(1) The higher direction of the laboratories in all matters
   of policy must be controlled by persons who are com-
   mercially minded.

(2) The principal scientists employed by the laboratories
   must be given adequate status and sufficient assurance
   that they will receive some share, however small, of the
   profits arising from their inventions.

I suggest that sufficient revenue to cover its expenses be
assured to the Research Company by way of retaining fees
from each Company in the Group or, if it is preferred, by one
retaining fee from the Parent Company. In addition I suggest
that royalties are assessed by the Board of Beechams Pills
Limited in its absolute discretion in respect of formulae or
processes evolved by the Research Company's laboratories and
made available to Group Companies. In providing for these

royalties it can be laid down that the Board will take into account the following factors, viz:—

(1) The value of each process or formula to the Company or Companies in the Group who are to use it.

(2) The period during which advantage will accrue. In the case of a patent, the period would, of course, automatically be the life of the patent.

Having settled the amount or rate of royalty and period during which it is paid to the Research Company, the Beecham Board would then decide what proportion, if any, should be allocated to one or more of the scientists employed by the Research Company who have contributed to the results achieved. I appreciate that this would present the Board with difficult problems but I can see no other way of assuring to the scientists proper return for their labour and I cannot conceive that we shall get enthusiastic co-operation from them unless we face up to the necessity of giving them an interest in the results of their inventions. Of course, I am only suggesting that royalties are allocated when some really original work is completed which results in a new preparation being put on the market by one or other of the Group Companies. Later on in this memorandum I recommend that the scientists in charge of each department should have a seat on the Board of the Research Company. I envisage that each one of these scientists should be eligible for a royalty allocation but I think that the Managing Director of the Company should be specifically excluded from any share in such royalties. I think this must be so because the Beecham Board will have to rely very largely on his impartial recommendations when making allocations to the other scientists.

I suggest that the Research Company should be departmentalised as set out hereunder. As I have pointed out earlier in this memorandum, Macleans Limited are already undertaking or arranging to undertake research work and in consequence are in a position to transfer a number of scientists who are qualified to control some of the departments. I mention their names and qualifications at the same time.

Pharmacological and Bacteriological Department

I am on the point of engaging Mr. Michael Chance as a Director of this department which as at present envisaged is being set up in Macleans Limited. Mr. Chance is a young man but he has considerable experience and ability. Professor Dodds has seen him and agrees with me that he is very suitable for the position.

Pharmaceutical Department

The type of work which would need to be carried out in this department has been undertaken in Macleans Limited by Dr. F. H. Milner. Dr. Milner is an able chemist and I think he is well qualified to direct this department.

Fine Chemicals Department

During the last 18 months we have employed in Macleans Limited Dr. H. R. Frisch of Vienna University. Dr. Frisch is a scientist of considerable distinction and I personally have formed a high opinion of his abilities. I believe that he would render very useful service in this department provided he was satisfied as to his participation in the profits arising from his inventions.

Toilet and Cosmetic Department

There is no-one at present in the employ of Macleans Limited who could be spared to direct the work of this department and it would be necessary for an outside appointment to be made unless Mr. Fabricius could spare Dr. Marriott.

Semi-scale production including plant and layout

This would probably be the most important department in the laboratories. I envisage it as being charged with translating laboratory results into practical large scale processes but it would also have to concern itself with the manufacturing processes already existing in the group factories, advising on improvements both to achieve greater technical excellence and economy.

I would like to see this department given into the charge of Mr. E. A. J. Koch who is already a Consulting Engineer to the

Group and who might be persuaded to give up his general consulting work in favour of a fulltime appointment on suitable terms.

I have given considerable thought to the constitution of the Board of the Company. It seems to me that we ought to be prepared to give the head of each department the status of a Director. Admittedly, if this is done it would not be possible to impose commercial control of the Research Company by means of a majority on the Board unless we were to appoint a very unwieldy Board. However, in practice the Board of the Research Company would have to take notice of any directions received from the Board of Beechams Pills Limited and this could be assured if the Articles were properly drawn.

It would be necessary to appoint a Managing Director of the Research Company, responsible for co-ordinating the work of the various departments and for maintaining liaison with Managers of Group Companies with regard to research and advice concerning formulae, processes and plant. I think it is essential that the person appointed to this position should be a practical man with technical qualifications and I have no hesitation in recommending Mr. W. McGeorge.

If this suggestion of mine is accepted it will mean that the technical staff of Macleans Limited will be very greatly depleted. I am assuming that the research work at present carried on in the Maclean factory will be transferred to the Research Company and also that Mr. McGeorge and Mr. Koch will be available to Macleans Limited for advice concerning formulae, processes and plant. Even so, it will be necessary to promote certain persons and we may experience difficulty until the war finishes when we shall have several able men due to return from the forces. Until that time comes, Mr. McGeorge might have to spend more of his time with us than one would consider desirable as a permanent measure.

I have dealt with what may be called the "permanent fulltime Directors" of the Company but I would like to make two points with regard to the remainder of the Board. I do not know whether Professor Dodds can allow his name to go on the Board of a Limited Company in view of his hospital appointment, but it may be that he would be able and prepared to do so. If so, his presence at the Board Meetings of the Company (which I envisage should be frequent and technical in character) would be of very great advantage.

Finally, I may say that I have always taken a very close interest in the research work carried on in the Maclean laboratories, and have formed a definite conclusion that there is advantage to be gained from the presence of a commercial man at these technical deliberations. I should be disappointed if I were not given an opportunity of joining the Board and thus maintaining this close association.

I have set out above the broad outlines of the scheme which I have in mind. It remains to deal with the location of the proposed laboratories and the important matter of capital equipment. In this connection we have to consider what is possible in wartime and what is desirable when peace returns. I do not think we shall get very far with this proposal in wartime unless we are able to obtain the support of one or more government departments. In spite of the prejudice which undoubtedly exists in most departments against the proprietary medicine trade, I think we should try to obtain this.

I think that the first laboratories should be set up in the offices and laboratory floor of the Amami factory next door to Macleans Limited. This would enable Mr. McGeorge to remain in close contact with the Maclean business during the war and it would also make it unnecessary for Mr. Koch to move his offices. There are available certain benches and services in the old Amami laboratory which could be utilised and we should not have to seek government permission to spend nearly so much money in setting up the organisation as we should do if we went elsewhere. Whether we should consider this as permanent home for the laboratories is another matter. Personally, I think that after the war the Research Laboratories should be set up in a separate building and two alternatives occur to me:—

(a) To build Beecham Research Laboratories on the site opposite the present Maclean factory or

(b) To obtain a large country house of suitable structure within reasonable distance of London and base the Research Laboratories at this house, building whatever additions and annexes are necessary.

There are attractions about both schemes which could be debated in due course.

It is only necessary at this juncture to put on record that besides facing an expenditure of something like £50,000 per annum we should be prepared to incur capital expenditure of at least a similar amount.

I have gone into some detail in putting forward my recommendations particularly with regard to the important personnel. It goes without saying that in addition to the scientists I have mentioned it would be necessary to employ a number of men and women with academic qualifications besides routine laboratory workers. The full number to achieve proper efficiency could obviously not be engaged during the war but I do think it is important that we should make a start now and in particular that we should make our strongest case to the Ministry of Health and the Ministry of Food for their support.

H.G.L.

5 *The End of the War —
and Afterwards*

Some time in 1943 Stanley Holmes (as he was then) saw me and said that Philip Hill was proposing to retire from the Chair of Beecham Group Ltd. and that he (Stanley Holmes) would succeed him. Mr Hill then proposed to appoint me Managing Director of Beechams. I enquired what was going to happen to Bernard Hobrow and was told that he would be invited to resign. However, Stanley Holmes said that he had represented to Mr Hill that I could not be spared from Macleans until the war was over and it had been agreed that my appointment should take place at the end of the war and that Stanley Holmes's nephew, Donald Parry, who was serving in the Army should, on his return, be appointed Assistant Managing Director. I noted this without much enthusiasm.

Then in August 1944 came Mr Hill's sudden death and all was confusion. The Secretary of Philip Hill & Partners Ltd. (the finance company through which Mr Hill controlled his many interests) said to me, 'As soon as the old man died all the performing seals got down off their little stools and started fighting one another'. Stanley Holmes became Chairman of the company and retained also the title Managing Director. He saw me and said that he did not want to make any other moves until the war had ended and we had dealt with its aftermath.

Stanley Holmes was very anxious to 'broaden the base' of the Group, and by this he meant becoming less dependent on medicines. In January 1945 he sent Dunbar and myself to see F. James (Newport) Ltd., which was a grocery business marketing a range of food items under the brand Nunbetta. With some shame I see from the Minutes that we recommended the purchase of the business as a means of introducing Group

59

products to the grocer. This is either a measure of our ignorance of the grocery trade at that time, or of our reluctance to cross swords with the Chairman.

Then in June 1945 Stanley Holmes proposed and secured the acquisition of C. & E. Morton Ltd. The Chairman of this company was Major-General J. Buckley, a friend of Holmes. Mortons had fallen on hard times and Buckley had been appointed to make an investigation and report to the Board. He had done so, recommended the dismissal of a number of executives, including the Chairman, and had then been offered the job himself! C. & E. Morton had started in business many years ago as general export merchants. They secured orders from overseas, particularly the Far East, and filled them in the early stages from other manufacturers but subsequently more and more from their own factories. The company had offices at Portsoken House, a factory at Millwall, and a fish-canning factory at Lowestoft where herrings were originally salted in barrels for the Scandinavian market and latterly canned. This business was dying and to take up the slack they had started to can peas.

Buckley was appointed to the Beecham Board in October 1946 and soon formed an alliance with Hobrow. The two of them proceeded to predict the demise of the proprietary medicines business, following the introduction of the National Health Service. They were helped in their campaign by the sales figures for Beechams' medicines, which were poor. I pointed out to the Board that the buoyant sales after the war were not all sold to the public but a lot went into retailers' and wholesalers' stocks which became very large. I knew this because of the Nielsen Reports that I received. Unfortunately, I predicted that these stocks would be worked off in six months, which proved to be optimistic, and with continued poor medicine sales Buckley and Hobrow were able to persuade the Board to approve their policy. This was to build up a chain of wholesale grocers and provision merchants designed to enable the grocer to compete with the co-operative societies! The whole thing was complete nonsense, but it was supported by Stanley Holmes, urged, I feel sure, by his desire to get away from the 'stigma' of 'patent medicines'. We acquired in quick succession:

Purnells Food Products Ltd.
W. H. Hart & Sons Ltd. with its subsidiaries:
  G. H. Kidson Ltd.
  A. F. Timmins Ltd.
John & James Tod & Sons Ltd. with its subsidiary:
  R. Garden Ltd.
R. W. Holden Ltd.
North of England Lard Refiners Ltd.

By this time I was becoming concerned about the future of the Group and I wanted to confine myself to running Macleans. My only other concern was Mac and research and because of this I acquiesced in appointments in which I had no interest. In 1947 Stanley Holmes offered me the position of Joint Managing Director with Hobrow, but I refused. I had little respect for the top management of Beechams and did not desire even to become Managing Director unless I could have full authority, which I was not likely to get. Following this, Stanley Holmes suggested that myself, Hobrow, and Gordon Dunbar (the Managing Director of Beecham Export Corporation) become Joint Managing Directors. I said that triple Managing Directors with no defined areas of responsibility was a nonsense and it was finally agreed that we became Joint Assistant Managing Directors which, of course, was also a nonsense, but I felt that I could not sulk in my tent any more without losing the power to support research. The Board Minute making these appointments proposed that accommodation should be provided for Dunbar and myself at Pall Mall and that in due course we should relinquish our appointments as Managing Directors of Macleans and Beecham Export Corporation respectively. I do not remember this and cannot believe that I ever intended to give up Macleans. I never did move to Pall Mall but then, as will be seen, my appointment and that of Dunbar only lasted six months.

Mac, with the help of Koch, had made great progress at Brockham Park and in spite of shortages everywhere had got the place equipped and working. Expenditure was running at the rate of £100,000 per annum but we were still floundering about with our basic policy.

Sir Charles Dodds had been appointed Chief Consultant at the outset and was working very closely with Mac. Apart from his great contribution to medical science he has, in my opinion, also earned the gratitude of his countrymen and his colleagues for another reason. In those days it was considered somewhat unethical for scientists to advise commercial firms and there were mutterings against Sir Charles, who thought that this was nonsense. He believed that industry and scientists should work together and himself undertook consultancy work for a number of companies, including Beechams, Ranks, Horlicks, and some American companies. I was told that in its inimitable snobbish fashion the scientific world called him E. Commercial Dodds (his full name was Edward Charles Dodds).

Sir Charles took no notice of all this and proceeded to persuade some of his colleagues to join him in advising Beechams. He urged us to offer worthwhile fees, substantially higher than those usually paid by those companies whose 'social' standing was such as to make them acceptable as consultees. We were only too ready to do so and I am sure that this made a big contribution to the gradual change in the attitude of many scientists to industry and their readiness to work with it. Of course, the fact that in consultation with such great names as Sir Charles, Sir Ernst Chain, and Sir Ian Heilbron, we made our wonderful discovery, also helped to change attitudes.

In December 1947, out of the blue, Stanley Holmes proposed to the Board a Committee to investigate research, consisting of Hubert Meredith (a Director of both Philip Hill & Partners and Beechams), Hobrow, and N. F. Fabricius. It was obvious that the Committee was going to be dominated by Hobrow. I went to see Holmes and asked him what Dunbar and I were doing as Assistant Managing Directors if we were not to be involved in such an enquiry and when I got no satisfaction, tendered him my resignation as Joint Assistant Managing Director. Dunbar also resigned. The work of the Committee was a disgrace. In the main it consisted of the sort of investigation in which Hobrow excelled, designed to unearth fraud. Dodds was accused of spending money in excess of his authority on payments to consultants and for investigations in outside laboratories, and Koch and Mac also came under intense scrutiny.

There was little I could do at the time and the Committee finally put in a report. They were unable to find any evidence of misfeasance and had to content themselves with oblique attacks on wasteful and extravagant expenditure. A number of recommendations were made and implemented. One was that Koch was asked to resign from the Board of Research and revert to his old position of Consultant to Macleans, County Laboratories, and research. Under another, a Committee was set up (to which I was appointed) to approve projects, review and recommend expenditure, and determine the method of charging research to companies. Quite clearly, research was not going very far and too many people had a finger in the pie, some by no means friendly. However, by 1949, Buckley and Hobrow had raised their sights.

In due course I was invited to attend a meeting at the head-quarters of Philip Hill & Partners Ltd. in St James's Street with Sir Brian Mountain, Stanley Holmes, Hubert Meredith, and Hobrow. It very soon became clear that it had already been decided to appoint Buckley Managing Director and that the meeting was for the purpose of placating me or involving me in the decision, if it were possible. I said that I would support Buckley's appointment wholeheartedly on one condition. This was that they transferred Beecham Research Laboratories to Macleans and left it entirely under my control. I said that Macleans would meet the whole cost and that I hoped to demonstrate that the expenditure would in due course pay off. This was agreed to and we all left the meeting in a happy frame of mind. I was able to undertake to meet the cost of research because I knew by then that Lucozade would yield increasing profits. I therefore made Lucozade a subsidiary of Beecham Research Laboratories Ltd., and obtained the approval of the Board to sell a number of B.R.L. shares to Mac and Dodds. I pointed out that this would provide an incentive to the two men on whom the success of research most depended.

I was surprised at how readily the Board accepted my rather shallow reasoning. My real objective was firstly to eliminate the sore thumb of a great red figure against Beecham Research Laboratories Ltd. by including Lucozade profits, and then to compensate Mac and Dodds for the indignities to which they had been subjected. I was sure that Lucozade profits would swamp the cost of research and that their shares would later on be worth a lot more than they paid for them.

The next two years were difficult ones for Beechams. I stayed out of the political cut and thrust which culminated in an attack on Stanley Holmes. Buckley had a two-year contract and towards the end of that time he and Hobrow lobbied the other Directors and convinced themselves that they could muster a majority on the Board to force the retirement of Stanley Holmes and the appointment of Buckley as Chairman.

In 1949, Sir Brian Mountain retired from the Board and his place was taken by Kenneth Keith, who in effect represented not only Eagle Star and Philip Hill but also the other institutions. I asked Kenneth to have lunch with me to gain his support for something I wanted the Beecham Board to approve (I forget what). At this lunch Kenneth suddenly said, 'Leslie, what would be your conditions for accepting the Managing Directorship of Beechams?' I said that I did not particularly want the job but that I realized that my choice was ultimately to leave the Group or to tackle the mess. I also said that I did not want to work with Stanley Holmes as Chairman and that I could not work with Hobrow. Kenneth said that he was speaking on behalf of Eagle Star and Philip Hill. They had produced figures which persuaded them that, taking inflation into account, Beechams were going downhill rapidly. This could not be allowed to continue and if I were prepared to take the job under Stanley Holmes's Chairmanship, he would guarantee me a free hand. Somewhat reluctantly, I agreed.

There was quite a fuss over getting rid of Buckley. Hobrow went quietly enough on generous terms but J.B. showed fight. He was quite fearless and I liked him because of his cheerful buccaneering spirit. I was called up to Stanley Holmes's office (he was senior partner in a firm of accountants with offices on the fourth floor of 68 Pall Mall, at that time the Beecham headquarters), and found J.B. there gaily making quite serious accusations against Holmes and saying he was going to law. After listening for a time I said, 'J.B. when you were proposed as Managing Director, I said that I would support you and I think you must agree that I have done so. Now it is your turn. You must know that you are finished and I think you should return the compliment and make life easier for me.' Immediately, J.B. changed. He said, 'Leslie, I think that you are right and I will go quietly for you – but not for him'. From then on everything went smoothly. Buckley and Hobrow departed, I was formally appointed Managing Director on 1 May 1951 and my other close associate, John Rintoul, joined the Board and followed me to Pall Mall. I also proposed the appointment of S. J. Graham as Personnel Director. The Board of Beechams then comprised:

Sir Stanley Holmes	Chairman
H. G. Lazell	Managing Director
W. McGeorge	Research and Technical Director
John Rintoul	Administrative Director
N. F. Fabricius	County Laboratories Ltd.
S. J. Graham	Personnel Director
Non-Executive	
Kenneth Keith	Philip Hill & Partners Ltd.
Hubert Meredith	Philip Hill & Partners Ltd.
Sir Arthur Marshall	The famous K.C.

John Rintoul had joined Macleans as a trainee before the war and in due course became my assistant. He was transferred to County Laboratories as Secretary in May 1940 and within three months he had joined the Army. He quickly became Adjutant to an artillery regiment, but so that he could remain with his regiment when it was ordered overseas he relinquished his appointment as Adjutant (it had something to do with a War Office requirement that Battalions proceeding overseas had to have a regular officer as Adjutant). The regiment arrived in Java just in time to be taken prisoner by the Japanese and he spent the rest of the war in prison under appalling conditions, which undoubtedly brought about his untimely death later on. On his return he became Administrative Director at Macleans and finally joined me at Pall Mall. His promotion to the Beecham Board was, of course, meteoric but I needed him badly. He subsequently described himself, in his inimitable fashion, as my dog's-body. A pessimist who mostly looked on the black side, he acted as a foil for my perennial optimism, brought order on to the scene, was very popular, and set an example of loyalty and integrity which was of immense value to the business and to me.

I met S. J. Graham in 1941 when he was at the Board of Trade. At that time Lord Beaverbrook was Minister of Aircraft Production and he was grabbing factories all over the place. One day a group of his people appeared at Macleans and demanded that we vacate the factory as they wanted it as a warehouse. We had rented a warehouse in nearby Harrow that had as large a floor space as we had at Brentford and, in my opinion, was a better warehouse and we offered this instead. However, Beaverbrook's boys said that we could move there, in spite of the fact that it would entail moving all our machinery, pipework, boilers, etc. I therefore appealed to the Board of Trade.

As a result of the outcry over some of 'the Beaver's' actions, it had just been decided that before a factory could be taken over, the Board of Trade must approve and the man in charge of this operation was S. J. Graham. He immediately took our side and refused to permit the occupation of Macleans but offered to approve the take-over of our warehouse. This came about and a few months later the warehouse was bombed and with all its stock went up in smoke! I had been very impressed by Graham's ability and courage in tackling Beaverbrook and when the war ended offered him a job at Macleans, where he dealt with Government Departments over many matters, including the allocation of glucose.

I had, for a long time, held the view that the personnel function should be represented on the Board. Directors in their enthusiasm for growth or in pursuit of profit, can often overlook the interests of the staff and I felt that there should be one Director charged with the interests of the employees. Thus I asked the Board to appoint Graham Personnel Director and he became the first of the line in Beechams and one of the first in British industry. After he retired, I brought Philippa Lane from Macleans as Personnel Controller. I could not ask the Board to appoint her a Director until she had proved herself but in 1961 she was elected to the Board and became one of the first woman Directors to be appointed to the board of a public company.

The personnel function rested on three main factors:

(1) The department was responsible for new appointments in both factory and offices, including top administrative appointments. For factory and office appointments this was turned over to personnel offices in Divisions. Top administrative appointments always had to be made through headquarters. Just as appointments had to be made through Personnel, so all dismissals had to go through that department. Management could only recommend dismissal to Personnel.

Personnel Division maintained liaison with various sources for staff including the universities, but we never relied exclusively on the universities. I wanted to get a good mix of people and was most anxious that where possible we should promote from the ranks.

(2) Welfare was an important factor. In the early days at Macleans, before the term 'personnel' came in use to indicate a wider function, we had a Welfare Officer. There we wanted everyone to feel that they 'belonged' and we endeavoured to achieve this by encouraging sports clubs, works councils, and by making 'news' available. We were also one of the first companies to introduce the five-day week and under the influence of Lord Amery, when he became Chairman, we were the first company to institute family allowances. By the time I moved to Beechams as Managing Director, the function had widened to 'personnel' and I established this at headquarters with Personnel Managers in every subsidiary operation. We made several attempts to publish magazines but none of them lived for long. Personnel

Division also administered the profit participation scheme and the two pension schemes, of which more anon.

(3) Finally, I relied on the Personnel Director to keep me up to date with the way staff were thinking and reacting. I was particularly anxious that I should know when anyone was in trouble and we often stepped in to help in cases of hardship. This was of great importance in fostering morale. In big companies the rule book and precedent oppresses everyone and only the chief executive can bend the rules and make some special provision. There were many cases and I can quote one where an employee was killed in a car accident. We immediately stepped in and made an allowance to the widow until we could put her affairs in order and determine that her death benefits from our pension scheme were adequate. This not only helped the widow but also morale generally.

The Personnel intelligence function became very important. Many executives who would not tackle me personally would go to Personnel (this was mainly in the days of Philippa Lane and her successor, Jack Smartt) and unburden themselves, knowing that I would hear about it. I used to make it clear to both Philippa and Jack that I *expected* them to be frank with me and on no account to co-operate with those who wished to keep knowledge away from me. No doubt they did not always do as I asked but I think that they told me everything they thought good for the business.

The pension schemes were in existence from the very early days. When Macleans, County Laboratories, and Eno were acquired, all these companies had better arrangements than Beechams and this caused the whole matter to be reviewed. We sought the advice of Noble Lowndes & Partners and as a result Beechams was one of the first companies to have a 'top hat' pension scheme for its senior executives entirely free of cost to the executive. This gave all those with twenty years' service or more when they retired at age 65, pensions of two-thirds of their salary at age 60. Then the rest of the staff were offered mem-

8. The late Duchess of Kent talking to a 70-year-old wartime shift worker at the Macleans factory. This was her first public visit following the tragic death of her husband.

9. Brockham Park from the air in 1971. The original house (*top right*) contrasts with the numerous additions following the penicillin discovery.

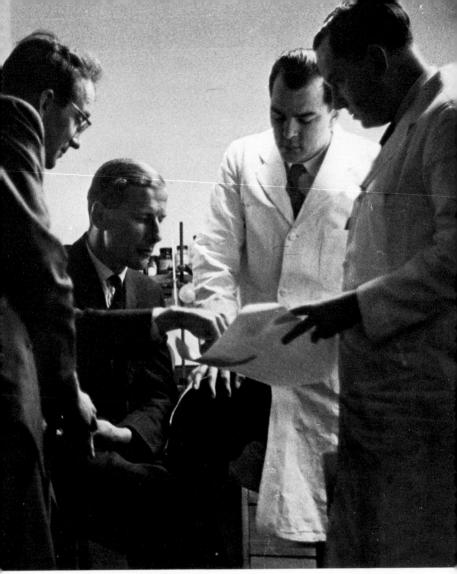

10. The scientists who isolated 6–APA, leading to the production of the new penicillins: (*from left*) F. P. Doyle, G. N. Rolinson, Dr. F. R. Batchelor, and Dr. J. H. C. Naylor.

11. Sales of the new penicillin, Penbritin, became far larger than any other Beecham brand. Two girls here closely inspect capsules before packing.

12. Syringes being filled with active pollen vaccine in sterile conditions. Beechams has been active in prescription medicines since 1949.

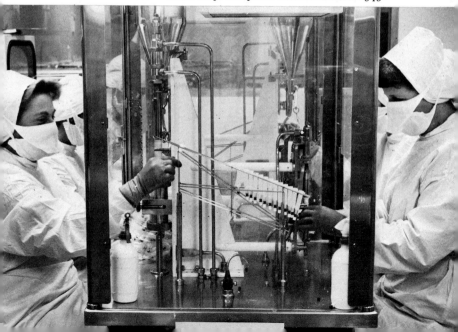

13. The first penicillin plant installed at Worthing.

bership of another scheme on a contributory basis which, with adequate service, could give them a pension of 50 per cent. In due course I persuaded the Board to make this scheme entirely free to the staff so that we could include everyone. Finally, we took out an insurance policy which provided widows of executives who had retired on pension a payment of approximately half that being made to their husband, if the husband died first.

The profit participation scheme was started by John Buckley. He was a great believer in profit participation but did not get his figures right. He completely ignored the need to finance future capital requirements and failed to appreciate the effects of continued inflation. The scheme he introduced, and persuaded the Board to accept, provided that 20 per cent of all profits above a base of roughly the existing figure should be appropriated to staff. The scheme had only been running for a year by the time I became Managing Director and I realized that it had to be changed quickly if we were to avoid trouble first with the shareholders and then inevitably with the staff.

In July 1952 I therefore proposed a new scheme under which a sum equal to 15 per cent of the excess of the gross ordinary dividend for the year over a datum was appropriated to the Profit Sharing Fund. Every year this fund was shared amongst all permanent employees (with over two years' service), including Executive Directors, in proportion to earnings. It was remarkable that this scheme stood up to both the rapid expansion and also the many take-overs that came about in the next eighteen years. Only when we acquired Thomas & Evans Ltd. with 5,660 employees, which included 1,150 van salesmen, did we have to modify it by increasing the percentage share-out.

There are many arguments about profit participation schemes and John Rintoul always cast doubts on the usefulness of ours. I personally thought that it all depended on what we expected from it. Probably John was right in arguing that it really did not provide much incentive but it seems to me that somehow the staff should share in the prosperity of the company. Any scheme which attempts to do this helps them to feel that they belong and associates them more closely with the executives who are running the business.

6 *We Get Going*

At 31 March 1951 Beechams' profits before tax were shown as £2,740,000, one and a half million from the home market and one and a quarter from overseas. The principal companies were:

(1) County Perfumery Co. Ltd. (name changed to County Laboratories Ltd. in 1954) run by N. F. Fabricius and marketing Brylcreem, the Silvikrin range of hair care products, the Amami products, and Hiltone Bleach.

(2) Macleans Ltd., which had been run by me, marketing Macleans Tooth Paste, Lucozade and Bristow's Lanolin Shampoo; also some medicines, including Macleans Stomach Powder, Fynnon Salt, and Mac Brand Antiseptic Throat Sweets.

   Associated with Macleans was C. L. Bencard Ltd., acquired in 1949 as a medium for building an 'ethical' pharmaceutical business. This company was managed by Douglas Stafford who was to lead our drive into the explosive ethical (or prescription) pharmaceutical market with the new penicillins.

(3) Beechams Pills Ltd., St Helens, managed by Joe Davies with Bill Ambrose as his close associate, marketing the Group's proprietary (or advertised) medicines originating with that company and the Veno Drug Co. Ltd. The most important were Beecham's Powders and Phensic.

(4) The 'Watford Group' comprising J. C. Eno Ltd., Yeast-Vite Ltd., the Iron Jelloid Co. Ltd., Phosferine (Ashton & Parsons) Ltd., Dinneford & Co. Ltd., and a few smaller companies. This group was managed by Mark Patten.

(5) C. & E. Morton Ltd., run by Mike Spry, controlling the grocery interests, including the wholesalers.

Overseas there was the Harold F. Ritchie Ltd. in Canada, which sold Eno's and Brylcreem. In the U.S.A. there was Eno-Scott & Bowne Inc. and there were companies in many parts of the world, mainly Eno companies with a few originating with Beechams and Macleans. These were controlled by various home companies, mainly J. C. Eno Ltd. but some by Macleans. In due course, all but the Western Hemisphere companies were put under the direction of the Beecham Overseas Department at Pall Mall, overseen by John Rintoul, which became Beecham Overseas Ltd. in 1955.

In reporting the position in those days I am dealing solely with actual control. In fact the legal company position was much more complex.

Profits were divided roughly as follows:

	Home (£'000)	Export & overseas (£'000)	Total £'000
Macleans	495	100	595
County Perfumery	223	215	438
Beecham Northern	494	91	585
Watford	127	182	309
Food Wholesalers	146	–	146
Mortons	45	152	197
Overseas Companies		470	470
Beecham Group Total	1,530	1,210	2,740

Profits on goods exported were substantially overstated as these were shown gross, without deduction of any overheads.

Morale gave me some concern on taking over as Managing Director. It was good in Macleans and County, where they had been successful, but bad everywhere else. I do not suppose that executives in the old companies much appreciated finding themselves responsible to me. The business had been going nowhere. Buckley had 'fired' a number of people (with considerable justification) and managers were on the defensive. I first of all announced that I would issue no directives from

Headquarters but would take the chair at a Management Committee Meeting to be held once a month at every company's headquarters. The companies were to hold Executive Committee Meetings every week with the Chief Executive in the chair and the Minutes of these meetings were dispatched quickly to myself, John Rintoul, and Mac. We (through John Rintoul) carefully defined the matters to be dealt with at Executive Committees and those to be dealt with at Management Meetings.

Overseas was split up. Right from the start I separated the Western Hemisphere (U.S.A., Canada, and South America) from the rest and made the managements there personally responsible to me. I had the same basic arrangements except that Management Meetings were only held when I was the other side of the water. For some time control was effected through Bob Alexander as President of Beecham (Canada) Ltd., which was set up in Toronto as a management company. Gradually I went mainly to New York and held management meetings there. I used to fly out three or four times a year and, in addition, Bob Alexander came to London. The rest of the world was left under the control of the various home companies until 1953 when the Beecham Overseas Department took over.

When Macleans acquired Beecham Research Laboratories in 1949, I had set up a Research Executive Committee at which I took the chair. This Committee continued to function and included myself, Mac, Sir Charles Dodds, and the head of research, Dr Farquharson. In due course Doug Stafford was also brought in and he was encouraged to visit Brockham at frequent intervals. We concerned ourselves principally with reviewing results, determining what work should be dropped, and approving new projects. It must be remembered that in those days and right up to the time of the great discovery, Research operated on a tight overall budget. There was no question of making a case for new work involving more expenditure. We had to keep within the budget and something had to be cut before anything new could be attempted. I remember in the early days complaining to Dr Farquharson that the lawns around the main house at Brockham Park were full of weeds and he reminded me that if he bought weed killer something would have to be saved from the research budget! I believe that the fact that we were working on a tight budget sharpened our thinking, kept us on our toes, and encouraged our best men to work on our most worthwhile projects.

It is interesting to recall those days. In 1949 the Beecham dividend had been cut. When I became Managing Director in 1951, the Ordinary Shares were selling to give a return of 9 per cent. Nothing would help us gain the confidence of the City until we could show a steady growth in profits and dividends. Our life blood was advertising but at St Helens this had been steadily cut so as to maintain profits. Fortunately, management had been afraid to increase prices and there was considerable scope in this area to find more money for advertising. Increased proprietary medicine profits would have to wait on increased sales.

However, the position was different in the case of Brylcreem. This product dominated the British hairdressing market, holding over 40 per cent of sales. N. F. Fabricius was primarily a marketing man and he was obsessed by 'share of market'. Nielsen did not help because all their statistics emphasized 'share'. Now the Brylcreem profit in the U.K. was a very low percentage of turnover and I pointed out to Fab that this really was not good enough because (a) it made his business very vulnerable if sales fluctuated and (b) it did not provide him with funds to develop new business, particularly shampoos. His reply was that if he increased price it would enable competitors to put rival creams on the market. We both knew that the Americans were anxious to do this but that they could not get down to our costs. However, I insisted that I would prefer to make a higher profit on a lower share of market and finally Fab gave way and put his prices up. This was very helpful to Beechams in the early days and, with Lucozade, helped our first profit increase in the year ended 31 March 1953. In the event both Colgate and Vaseline put out imitation products and Vaseline took a modest share of the market but Brylcreem held its own and from that day on became an increasing contributor to Group profits.

73

Then we had the problem of the grocery wholesalers and the overseas canning companies purchased in the Buckley era. In Britain we had John & James Tod of Edinburgh; F. James and Nunbetta Products of Newport; and Hart & Sons, predominantly meat wholesalers, in the Midlands. None of these companies were making profits showing a reasonable return on investment. Overseas there was Henry Williams in Australia and the Wolseley Fruit Canning Co. of South Africa. I felt that getting involved in all these was a mistake but how to get out without loss?

We managed to sell the overseas companies at acceptable prices, but the British wholesalers were not making enough profit to justify anything like the price they stood at in our books. Mike Spry, who was then running Mortons and its satellite companies, pointed out that net assets were actually in excess of book value. These net assets consisted very largely of debtors and stocks. He suggested that it would be possible slowly to reduce operations, cutting out unprofitable segments, reducing the area of country catered for and finishing up either by winding up the business altogether, or in possession of a slimmer company still making a profit which could be sold for a much reduced price. This he did most cleverly. Some were eventually wound up and Tods, after it had been 'slimmed', was sold to Bernard Hobrow's son who, I am pleased to say, did very well with it.

Macleans presented a problem. It was a multiple-product business, operating in three very different markets. First of all, there were the medicines which depended on their advertising. Then there were the toiletry products including Macleans Tooth Paste and Bristow's Lanolin Shampoo and, finally, we had Lucozade. I realized that such a business would demand management of higher calibre and I did what I could to reduce the complexity. Douglas Stafford was answerable directly to me for C. L. Bencard Ltd. I then separated Lucozade under its own management and made it report directly to me. Finally, I promoted the Sales Director of Macleans to the position of Managing Director, confident that at Pall Mall I could keep a close eye on the business and make up for any management deficiency. This was a mistake that I continued to make right through my business life. I never did succeed in bolstering an inadequate top manager either by giving more of my own time to him or by appointing able people to support him.

Macleans started to get into trouble with the tooth paste and I soon had to make management changes. We never succeeded in achieving adequate management for Macleans and eventually in 1959, when we needed the factory for Beecham Research Laboratories Ltd. and our new penicillins, I seized the opportunity to simplify management functions by breaking up the company. The toiletry products were transferred to County Laboratories, thus founding the Group Toiletry Division, and the advertised medicines to St Helens, founding the Group Proprietary Medicine Division. This meant that each management team only had one type of product to deal with. Even so, the County team for some time found it difficult to deal with tooth paste, competing as it did with the big 'soapers' Colgate and Unilever, who were so strongly entrenched with the grocers. The grocer was used to 'deals' on soaps and responded readily when tooth paste was included. Thus he cut price in return for special discounts and carried 'offers' to the public of free tooth brushes and other items with one or more tubes of tooth paste. Our selling power to the grocers was much lower than that of the big 'soapers' and we had to wait until 1966, when Beecham Products Division was set up under Ronnie Halstead, before we were able to compete on more equal terms.

Research and the ethical pharmaceutical business presented the big problem. Doug Stafford could make little real headway with C. L. Bencard Ltd. and whenever we discussed his business he would remind me that he was waiting for something to come out of research. On the other hand, the more we learnt about pharmaceutical research, the greater the odds against us seemed to become. Our expenditure was running at the rate of £100,000 per annum. We were competing with many U.S. and European companies spending more than twenty times that sum.

The only answer so far as I could see was to concentrate our work into a narrow field. Sir Charles Dodds recommended that we concentrate on the amino-acids. These 'bricks' in the structure of protein seemed to present an opportunity for a number of specifics, particularly in the field of geriatrics. We did a lot of work in this area but we never took very drastic action to concentrate our efforts. No one could produce a strong enough case for any one particular area, and it needed absolute conviction before we could be ruthless enough. Meanwhile, I realized that we would have to maintain a very strict limit on our annual research expenditure and it was made perfectly clear to everybody that the budgeted allocation was the absolute limit in every year. The carrot was, of course, that once we had a marketable discovery more money would automatically become available. This was so because we arrived at our budget by taking a fixed percentage of all medicine sales. Prescription medicines were charged $7\frac{1}{2}$ per cent and advertised proprietaries were levied $2\frac{1}{2}$ per cent.

Joe Davies came to me to complain that research was not working in areas likely to help his advertised products and he asked why he should have to make this contribution. I had to tell him that in the first place it was his contribution to the future of Beecham Group, and in the second place it was his contribution to the welfare of his customers. We had a duty to the future of the company, even if this meant sacrificing profits that would redound to our immediate credit. We also had a moral duty to the public to allocate some of the profits from our advertised medicines to the furtherance of pharmaceutical knowledge, at least until we had sufficient pharmaceutical sales to enable us to charge them with the cost.

And so at Pall Mall we all started our long round of company Management Meetings in England and the Western Hemisphere. John and Mac came to all the Meetings in the U.K., Mac sometimes accompanied me to the Western Hemisphere, and he spent a lot of time at Brockham Park, now run by John Farquharson.

7 St Helens

St Helens was where everything started many years ago. Thomas Beecham was born in 1820 and he first sold Beecham's Pills in a market at Wigan in 1842. His business prospered and he moved to St Helens in 1858, building a modern factory there in 1887. The ornate entrance hall and staircase is very much as it was then, but the factory itself has been altered and extended first in 1934, then in 1948, and again in 1956.

Thomas Beecham retired in 1895 (and died in 1907). He was succeeded by his son, Joseph Beecham, who was knighted in 1912, created a Baronet in 1914, and died in 1916. Sir Thomas Beecham, the famous conductor, was Sir Joseph's son. Both father and son were interested in music and in due course, Beechams Pills Ltd. bought Covent Garden, where Thomas was involved in rescuing British Opera. When Sir Joseph died, the business was carried on by the Executors. Sir Thomas was only interested in music and all the money he could get was swallowed up in the pursuit of his passion. Curiously enough, it was during this period that Beecham's Powders were first launched (1926).

The business got into financial difficulties which, I was told, were due to losses at Covent Garden and in 1927 Philip Hill, in association with Louis Nicholas, a Liverpool Chartered Accountant, came to the rescue with an arrangement which bought out the family, who ceased from that date to have any connection with the business. Philip Hill had purchased for £1·7 million part of the settled estates of Lord Derby and he agreed to sell these estates at cost to Beecham Estate & Pills Ltd. in exchange for the Pill business. The name of the Estate company was then changed to Covent Garden Properties Co. Ltd. and in 1928 Beechams Pills Ltd. was formed to own the Pill business. Shares in both companies were then offered to the public and the family were paid off. Philip Hill, of course, took his profit in shares in the companies, this profit accruing to his finance company, Philip Hill & Partners Ltd. The original directors of Beechams Pills Ltd. were Philip Hill, Sir Arthur Marshall, K.C., Louis Nicholas, Henry Gregory (manager of the Veno Drug Co. Ltd.), Austin Scott and C. T. Scrymgeour, manager and advertising manager, respectively, of the Pill business.

Beechams owned practically all the Ordinary Shares of the Veno Drug Co. Ltd., makers of Veno's Cough Mixture, which company had a factory and offices at Manchester. Almost immediately, Louis Nicholas, who acted as Managing Director of Beechams Pills Ltd. in fact if not in name, put through a very curious arrangement under which Austin Scott and C. T. Scrymgeour moved from St Helens to Manchester. Responsibilities of the directors of the two businesses were divided as follows – Henry Gregory was responsible for factories; Austin Scott was in charge of the whole office organization including accounting, and C. T. Scrymgeour controlled the advertising of both companies. Beechams Pills Ltd. acted as sole selling agents for Veno on the following terms:

(1) Both companies carried on their Works, each keeping separate books of account.

(2) Beecham acted as *del credere* selling agents for Veno and were paid a commission on sales.

(3) Veno advertising expenditure was mutually agreed by the Boards of both companies.

(4) Beechams was given the use of Veno's Manchester office and provided the necessary office staff for both companies and the sales organization.

This arrangement persisted until 1931 and I understood that there was constant bickering and trouble, which one would certainly expect. When Stanley Holmes joined the Board following the purchase of Yeast-Vite, he was made Joint Managing Director with Louis Nicholas, and he quickly influenced a decision to terminate the complex arrangements. Both managements resumed their separate identity and it was not until

General Buckley was made Managing Director in 1949 that the two businesses were completely merged under one management at St Helens. By this time all the old managers had died or retired and J. H. Davies was appointed Managing Director.

Joe Davies was operating at a considerable disadvantage. He and his executive were very badly paid, did not possess the standing to argue with anyone and, in consequence, were kicked around. George Royds, the advertising agent for Beechams Pills Ltd., who had been a friend of Philip Hill, would not visit St Helens but demanded that they visit him in London. It is no doubt advantageous to hold certain meetings at the offices of the agent but the decision should be made by management and not by the agent. Royds considered that he had a right to the Beechams business and certainly St Helens management would not have dared to sack him.

Profits had not been buoyant for some time and, what was worse, advertising expenditure was at an all-time low. On a number of occasions for the purpose of maintaining profits, and on the instructions of Stanley Holmes, advertising had been cut and in relation to a number of brands was clearly inadequate. Prices had not been increased since before the Second World War and margins were badly eroded. Because of this, cartons and leaflets had not been reintroduced after the war, and all their products looked cheap.

When I paid my first visit to St Helens as Managing Director of the Group I found Davies apprehensive and waiting for more blows to descend on him. He no doubt wondered which way he would be blown by this new change in top control. There was really nothing wrong with the ability of management there. It was quite capable of dealing with its very specialized business. What it needed was confidence and the first thing I did was to increase top salaries and, indeed, to pursue a steady policy of substantial annual increases until they had reached an adequate level. Then I proposed that they increase all prices, put their products back in redesigned cartons, and in many cases increase advertising expenditure. Fears were expressed that increased prices would still further depress sales and I said that I was quite prepared to take personal responsibility for this. Finally, I told George Royds that if he wished to keep the account, he must be prepared to visit St Helens when asked. There were no dramatic results from this action but things looked healthier.

The dramatic results came when I made a much more fundamental proposal in 1953. Beecham's Powders had become a substantial brand in the analgesic market. They were advertised for headaches and rheumatic pains during most of the year but during the winter they were advertised for colds and flu. It was clear that the public had appreciated their value for colds because sales rose substantially during periods when they were prevalent. Phensic, on the other hand, had started life as a remedy for flu and was still heavily advertised during epidemics. At other times it was advertised for headaches and rheumatic pains. I proposed that advertising for Beecham's Powders be concentrated on colds during the twelve months of the year (including flu in the season) and that Phensic be advertised solely for headaches. Finally, I proposed that we take Phensic advertising away from Royds and give it to J. Walter Thompson.

I was first introduced to the idea of concentrating advertising on one point by Norman Moore of Bensons. They were making the one simple claim that Macleans Tooth Paste made teeth whiter, and Norman often resisted suggestions to widen the claims. Subsequently, I had observed that a number of successful products were selling on one simple claim. One example was Horlicks and 'Night Starvation' – another was Carters Little Liver Pills, which had used only one piece of copy for years. We were having great difficulty advertising Lucozade where the usage was so varied that we had not found one claim that we were prepared to concentrate on and I was coming more and more to the view that until we did, we would not progress as fast as I wished.

In regard to analgesics we knew from our consumer research that these remedies were used mainly for headaches and colds, with a third important area in rheumatism. Now aspirin, which was the main ingredient in most of the products used, together with phenacetin sometimes used as a secondary ingredient, were very effective drugs. Sir Charles Dodds was always telling me that aspirin was the first 'wonder drug', that it had practically no side-effects, and was very safe. The public certainly seemed to have found this out, for total national consumption was at a staggering level and going up every year.

The effectiveness of aspirin, I believed, had another result. It was very difficult and costly to build the sales of a new brand of analgesic. The public were very satisfied with the brand they were using and products like Aspro, Anadin, and Disprin were hard to shake. Phensic lost money for years before it became established and I had witnessed the tremendously costly fight to establish Bristol-Myers' Bufferin on the U.S. market. I felt therefore that the answer was to concentrate our claims, and make one only for each of our brands. Beecham's Powders obviously had to concentrate on colds. This was quite possible, for people caught cold at all times of the year. We could spend more in the winter than in summer and we could add 'and flu' at appropriate times. Anyway, Beechams was a most effective treatment for colds because it provided a small rapidly absorbed dose which could be taken frequently. Phensic, on the other hand, gave a more powerful dose and it seemed to me that this made it the most appropriate headache remedy. It is true that it had started life as a treatment for influenza and that when there was an epidemic sales of Phensic went up markedly. However, we were up against Anadin, a very similar formula, and they were outspending us by more than two to one. I felt that we could only compete effectively by concentrating. These ideas were put into effect in 1953 and I give overleaf graphs of sales and advertising for our two brands from 1949 to 1965.

The success of Beecham's Powders and Phensic put heart into the St Helens management and it continued to gain in confidence. In 1953 we had transferred some of the Watford Group medicines to them. These included Iron Jelloids, Thermogene Medicated Wadding for aches and pains, and Phosferine tonic. They had plenty of problems because there was a revolution going on in the proprietary medicine business. 'Tonics' were all losing sales, as were laxatives. On the other hand, analgesics and vitamin supplements were gaining and, of course, there was

81

FROM PILLS TO PENICILLIN

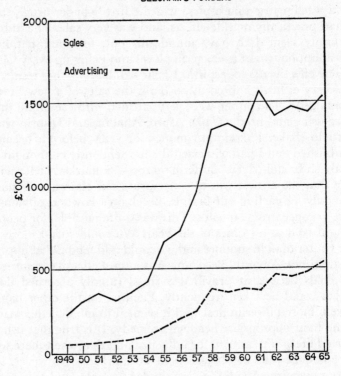

BEECHAM'S POWDERS

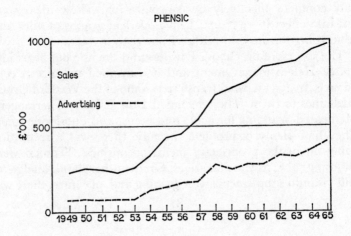

PHENSIC

the great increase in health drinks such as Ribena, PLJ, and Lucozade. Falling sales in some areas were attributed to the National Health Service, but I believe it was also caused by rising standards of education. Grossly exaggerated advertising no longer sold goods and to be believable copy had to stay close to the facts.

In 1959 St Helens took over Maclean Brand Stomach Powder, Eno's, Dinneford's Magnesia, Yeast-Vite, and Fynnon Salt from Macleans and became Beecham Proprietary Medicine Division. They continued thus until merged into the new Pharmaceutical Division set up in 1962 where their marketing group still functioned as a separate team. Finally in December 1966 advertised medicines were moved from the Pharmaceutical Division to the newly created Products Division. Marketing for this Division came under Don McLure with separate sections for Toiletries, Health Drinks, Proprietary Medicines, and Soft Drinks, all centred at Brentford. St Helens became a factory operation only, over which the ornate entrance hall and stairway brooded in silent recollection of past glories.

8 *County Perfumery Co. Ltd.*

Brylcreem was first marketed in 1928 by the County Chemical Co. Ltd. of Birmingham owned by Mr Wilfrid Hill and his family. Mr Hill had asked his Chief Chemist to formulate a new-style hair cream which would be different from the brilliantines, oils, and gums then in use. The result was 'Brylcreem', a new 'brilliantine cream' containing no gum or starch.

Brylcreem was originally sold only to hairdressers and up to 1935 no money had been spent on advertising. Instead tens of thousands of gallons were given free to hairdressers for use in their shops. At this time sales were at the rate of 40,000 bottles per week, say 2 million per annum compared with over 100 million per annum achieved in 1961.

In 1935 George Royds was appointed advertising agent and he stated his objectives thus: 'Our first aim was to secure the goodwill of the barber and at a later stage create a masculine image that would appeal to millions of everyday people – football fans, sportsmen, etc.'

Royds favoured continued concentration on the barber because 'wherever one shops for a hairdressing – at the chemist, stores, multiple or grocers – one must go to the barber to have one's hair cut. He has a captive audience and his views on matters relating to the hair can very easily influence the purchaser . . . he was the king pin on which to hang our campaign.'

Early advertising showed some everyday situations in a barber's shop. Then came the war and advertising concentrated on showing men in R.A.F. uniforms – the 'Brylcreem Boys'. At one time this became a descriptive term for 'R.A.F. types'.

After the war advertising moved to using well-known sportsmen. Dennis Compton, the famous cricketer and footballer, had an exclusive contract for some time and then many other well-known names were used. For a long time considerable attention was still paid to the hairdresser, but gradually sales moved first to the chemist and then to the grocer also.

N. F. Fabricius had managed Brylcreem since its inception and had been running County Laboratories Ltd. without much interference since its acquisition by Beechams in 1939 (as County Perfumery Co. Ltd.). Brylcreem was more and more dominating the hairdressings market, but the company also sold a large number of small brands like Hiltone Bleach, for women's hair, and Brylfoam, a cream shampoo in a tube. Then in 1949 Fab acquired the business of Drugs Ltd., which sold Pure Silvikrin. This was a lotion for treating thinning hair, addressed mainly to men but also used by women. It was high priced and sales in the U.K. were of the order of £75,000 per annum. There were a number of other products sold under the Silvikrin brand, such as shampoos and hairdressings, making a total turnover of about £250,000 per annum. Fab was not able to buy the world rights, the owner wanting to retain Europe and the U.S.A. for his company, which was based in Switzerland. With this business came A. E. V. (Bay) Houchen who was, in due course, to assume control of County, later to join the Beecham Board, and then to take charge of Beecham Foods.

During the war Fab had approached me to suggest that Macleans take the Nielsen Survey for Macleans Tooth Paste. This survey was produced every two months based upon a continuous audit of a statistically accurate sample of retail outlets. At that time Nielsen audited both chemists and grocer sales. Dr E. L. Lloyd of Nielsen – 'Doc' as we called him – came along to Macleans and made a 'presentation' showing charts which set out our sales and those of our competitors in various types of outlets. I took the Nielsen figures for Macleans sales and after making various adjustments, so that they were comparable, set them beside our own sales figures. They were pretty accurate and I concluded that if our competitors were so well informed about our sales, we had better learn as much about them. From that time on, the Nielsen figures, which showed also stocks in the hands of the trade and 'out of stock' positions, were one of my major marketing tools and the service was gradually taken throughout the Group. Doc Lloyd became a very good friend of mine. He was an Anglophile American and he introduced me to many others in wartime London, where they were working and living, mostly without their families, who had been sent back to the U.S.A.

In December 1947 the Amami business, which had been in continuous decline, was put under the control of Fab. It still had a range of powder shampoos (mostly based on soap) in *6d.* sachets which had to be mixed in water and then poured on to the hair. Doc Lloyd had shown us the Nielsen survey for shampoos which revealed that the market was growing rapidly and that Beechams only had a very small share. Fab and I therefore agreed that County and Macleans should get together and concoct plans to capture some more of this business for Beechams, and we set up technical and marketing meetings between our two executives. It was soon clear that the rivalry between Macleans and County was very strong, but Fab and I were not affected and the arguments that developed between our two laboratories proved beneficial. Macleans took its Bristow brand which had been acquired in March 1947 with a small toilet soap business, and put out Bristow's Lanolin Shampoo in a tube. This was very successful and in a relatively short time, took some 10 per cent of the market. County went after the liquid market and after acquiring Drugs Ltd. relaunched Silvikrin Liquid Shampoo as a green liquid based on a new detergent obtained from Marchon Products Ltd. This product was put up in bottles and small plastic single-dose sachets and also took about 10 per cent of the market. So in a relatively short time Beechams had seized a sizeable share and we all felt pretty pleased with ourselves.

Brylcreem, of course, dominated the County business and it was one of the five or six brands on which the growth of what was eventually to become our Proprietaries Division depended, but moving into the shampoo market was a most important step for us. It turned out that shampoos were at the beginning of a sustained period of growth throughout the whole of the Western World. For many years, in many countries, market increases in excess of 10 per cent per annum occurred and although patterns varied enormously from country to country, growth was the same everywhere. Then again, the sheer size of the market was so important. In the U.S.A. shampoos almost equalled dentifrice sales, and although this was not so in the U.K. they were very much larger than hairdressings.

One thing puzzled us. It appeared that no one brand could for long take much more than 10 per cent of the market. County in due course put out a whole range of Silvikrin Shampoos but could not break through the barrier for very long. When they assumed responsibility for Bristows they added a range there, but still could not get more than about 10 per cent for the brand. I puzzled about this for a long time and eventually came to the conclusion that we were dealing with a market where no one was able to produce a completely satisfactory product. Hair behaves very differently on different persons, in different climates and circumstances, and during different states of health. There are the problems of 'fly away' and greasiness and dandruff. Consequently, there was always reason for change and our market research told us that there were very few loyal users of any brand. This was also true of the U.S. market except that in due course Procter & Gamble were for a time able to reach a 20 per cent share with 'Head and Shoulders', a shampoo for dandruff. However, in the U.S.A. Procter & Gamble are able to deploy so much market power and spend so much money that they can usually make themselves the exception.

Therefore, when later on Bay Houchen came to me and said that he thought that we might be able to arrange a merger with Marchon Products, I was interested. Marchon had been started soon after the war by Frank Schon, a refugee. It was established in Cumberland and produced, among other things, a whole range of detergents. These were supplied to many companies for inclusion in shampoos and other products for washing fabrics and the like. If we were going to produce a shampoo which was demonstrably superior it would have to be because of the detergent used but at this point any improvement effected by Marchon would be available for everybody.

The position was complex. Colgate had a very big business with Marchon for they not only purchased detergent for shampoos but different grades for clothes washing powders and dishwashing powders and liquids. If Beechams acquired the business then it might well lose a number of customers who would not tolerate buying their principal raw material from one of their biggest competitors. Clearly, a decision to acquire would also mean a decision to go into the bulk detergent business and compete with Unilever and Procter & Gamble, perhaps in the clothes washing market and certainly in the dishwashing market.

We decided against and I can remember a number of reasons. Firstly, I did not think that we could expect to compete on equal terms with Unilever and Procter & Gamble in detergent research. They were spending very large sums of money competing with one another and I thought that we would eventually be killed if we joined in. Then, if we had negotiated a deal, Frank Schon would have joined our Board. I did not know him but, like me, he had a reputation as a stormy petrel and I thought we might disagree. Then the penicillin discovery had been made and we were facing a major effort to build a worldwide pharmaceutical business. I was afraid that a major effort in the grocery field was beyond our resources. It could be that I was wrong not to plunge in. Had we been successful there would have been plenty of growth potential for many years, but it would have again depleted our reserves in manpower and I doubt if we would have been able to provide adequate management.

So we did our best to produce better and distinctive shampoos and a good deal of time in the County Product Research Laboratories was spent in this area. Then in 1955 Bay Houchen asked to be allowed to buy Vosene Medicated Shampoo. This product had been put on the market by a retired Billingsgate fishmonger who had moved to Bury in Lancashire in 1946. Vosene was gaining market share in spite of the fact that it had little selling weight behind it and very little had been invested in advertising. Bay warned me that his laboratories had condemned the formula and had expressed the view that it was a bad shampoo. His opinion was that this could not be so and I agreed with him and recommended a purchase to the Board. In due course Vosene was added to our list. This gave us over 30 per cent of the shampoo market in the U.K. and Beechams now held the largest share. It is interesting to record that once Vosene became a Group product the County Laboratories looked on it with a kinder eye and eventually identified a principle which they concluded explained its superiority and which was applied to all our other shampoos!

Bay Houchen became Chairman of Beecham Foods Ltd. in 1959 and gave up County to Bob Murphy in 1960. In 1962 Macleans and County were merged and became Beecham Toiletry Division under Tony Fabricius with Bob Murphy as his Administrative Director. At this date we also created the Food and Drink Division and this became Bay's sole concern. I transferred him there because he had come up through advertising and marketing and I wanted to see whether he could tackle a business that needed administrative ability of a high order and where advertising was not all-important. This Division also controlled Coca-Cola and Pascalls (confectionery). Unfortunately, Bay could not accept the appointment of Doug Stafford as Executive Vice-Chairman in 1964, and resigned. This was a pity. He was not finding Food and Drinks an easy operation and I often asked myself what would have happened if I had left him in charge of the enlarged Toiletry Division, a job which would have given him no difficulties.

9 *The Watford Group*

The Veno Drug Co. Ltd. had been acquired by Beecham Estate & Pills Ltd. in 1925 and was included in the Beecham purchase by Philip Hill in 1928. Veno had a product called Dr Cassells Tablets which was advertised as a tonic. In due course its sales started to decline and the management concluded that this was principally due to Irving's Yeast-Vite, whose factory and offices were at Watford and whose sales and advertising were obviously increasing very fast. Yeast-Vite had been acquired by Stanley Holmes in association with the Berry brothers, later Lords Kemsley and Camrose, and Philip Hill approached them and negotiated a purchase on behalf of Beechams Pills Ltd.

One of the terms of this agreement was that Stanley Holmes should join Beechams as Joint Managing Director with Louis Nicholas, the Liverpool accountant and financier, who was a close associate of Philip Hill, and was the effective Managing Director of Beechams at that time. There developed a strong rivalry between the two which ultimately resulted in Louis Nicholas resigning as Joint Managing Director of Beechams and becoming Vice-Chairman, but concentrating more of his attention on Timothy Whites Ltd. and Taylors (Cash Chemists) Ltd., the chains of chemist shops of which he was Chairman and which at that time were important competitors of Boots.

In 1935 Beechams acquired Phosferine (Ashton & Parsons) Ltd., with a factory and offices at Watford. Phosferine was originally a homoeopathic product but it had subsequently been advertised. In 1936 The Natural Chemicals Co. Ltd. (Phyllosan) was purchased and attached to Ashton & Parsons. Then in 1942 Philip Hill bought the associated businesses of Endocrines-Spicer Ltd. and Harwoods Laboratories Ltd., whose factory and offices were also at Watford. It was this acquisition that brought Doug Stafford into the Group. All of these companies were grouped together after the war, together with J. C. Eno Ltd. and Dinneford & Co. Ltd., and put under the control of Arthur Mortimer, who had joined us on the Group Board from Government service. I must make it clear that in those days whilst companies were 'grouped' together they retained their separate entities, and some of them their separate managers, but they had a common Chairman who was supposed to exercise overriding control.

Mortimer had been Secretary of the National Pharmaceutical Union before the war and became Deputy Director of Medical Supplies at the Ministry of Supply during the conflict. Curiously he was Chairman of a Committee that refused to grant Professor Ernst Chain any facilities to develop the deep fermentation of penicillin. In the early days penicillin was produced by fermenting appropriate moulds and feed stock in thousands of bottles by means of surface culture. These bottles were held in racks which rocked to and fro. It was a frightfully expensive procedure and incapable of providing adequate supplies. Ernst accurately predicted that the proper method was by means of deep fermentation in very large vessels through which air was pumped. This method was already being applied to the production of citric acid and he requested that facilities be made available to develop a process for penicillin. When one considers that this was a request from the genius who had developed the process for extracting penicillin from the mould, it is amazing that the Committee should have refused it – but it did, and it was the Americans who developed deep fermentation and cornered the market. I believe that right up to the time that we discovered the new penicillins, every kilo of penicillin fermented in Britain yielded royalties to the U.S.A.

Nothing much happened to the Watford Group during Mortimer's time. The Eno home business was relatively small and Beecham Overseas, with Gordon Dunbar and Mark Patten, controlled most of the overseas companies. Then with the appointment of Buckley as Managing Director of the Group, Dunbar and Mortimer were sacked and Mark Patten was appointed Managing Director of J. C. Eno Ltd. Patten was an old Eno employee whose duties had previously been concerned with its overseas business. Beecham Overseas was broken up and control of the Eno overseas trading companies in the U.S.A., Canada, South Africa, Australia, South America, etc., reverted to Mark Patten as Managing Director of J. C. Eno. He still spent most of his time dealing with those companies. They were not in good condition, prices had not been increased, margins were inadequate, staff was underpaid and in some cases took bribes from suppliers to augment their income.

Buckley had cleared out some of the dead wood and had dealt with the bribery before I took over as Managing Director. I immediately assumed responsibility for the U.S.A., Canada, and South America but did not touch anything else overseas until 1953. However, Beecham Technical Division was set up in 1951–52. One of its major objectives was to ensure that products were manufactured in a uniform way in all overseas factories, and to set up local quality control.

At that time Eno's 'Fruit Salt' was our most important overseas brand. During a night-time air raid in September 1940, the Eno factory at New Cross in East London was set on fire by incendiary bombs and the next day was hit by an explosive bomb which killed a number of firemen at work on the fire. The Managing Director of Eno would not come up from Haywards Heath where the subsidiary Thermogene factory was situated, and Macleans were asked by Stanley Holmes to take over. Mac and Koch went down in 'tin hats' through quite serious raids and set about organizing the removal of what remained of the machinery and stock – quite a lot, having regard to the shambles the place presented. We manufactured Eno's 'Fruit Salt' at Brentford for the rest of the war and thus was born the work that enabled the salt to remain stable and free-flowing.

When in 1940 Mac and Koch took a look at the Eno process they were contemptuous. They considered it old-fashioned and unscientific. In particular they were highly amused at a procedure adopted when the mixture would not flow properly in the mixing drum. This was to take a bicycle pump, draw in water, and squirt it into the moving drum! No one knew why this worked, but it did. However, the salt was never truly stable and it was filled into narrow-necked bottles closed with special corks cut with the grain running lengthwise. This was supposed to let the gas, generated by the continuing reaction between tartaric acid and sodium bicarbonate, escape.

Mac decided to make Eno's by a simpler, more up-to-date process, and the result was catastrophic – all the salt setting hard in the bottles. We had therefore to return to the old process but he remitted the problem to our laboratories. The work went on in a desultory fashion and passed to Beecham Research Laboratories when they were set up. In due course the answer was found and research announced that they could stabilize Eno's so that it remained free-flowing. They pointed out, however, that with the stabilized salt it was better to have an absolutely airtight seal.

When I became Managing Director I found that Canada were not using the standard cork in the Eno bottle but a bayonet screw-on cap with a special valve-like wad that was supposed to let gas escape but prevent the ingress of moisture. They were also experimenting with a wide-mouth bottle that had the same type of cap and wad and which allowed the insertion of a spoon to take up a dose of the salt. With the standard bottle the salt had first to be poured into the palm of the hand. Patten was dead against all this, contending that the public would use damp spoons and thus cause more trouble with hardened salt. I insisted that we start market tests in England and then Mac told me of the success at Brockham, which meant that we could go ahead with ordinary simple wads which were airtight.

The stable Eno's in the wide-mouth bottle and the single-dose envelope pack were great successes and the brand was steadily updated throughout the world. Sales increased substantially in Canada, South Africa, and Australia but failed to develop a big business in the U.K. or the U.S.A.

Besides fighting me over the Eno bottle Patten led the Eno old guard in resisting a major change in branding. Years prior to Beechams taking over, the Eno Directors had consulted

Sir Stafford Cripps (who was a barrister and had married one of the Eno daughters) about their rights to the trade mark 'Fruit Salt'. He had delivered a written opinion, which became an Eno Bible, that laid down how to retain exclusive rights to the words 'Fruit Salt'. What was in effect a descriptive term must *only* be used as a trade mark and the word Eno must *never be so used*. The pack was covered in wrapping paper festooned with grapes on which the words 'Fruit Salt' appeared in large type and 'Eno' down below in small type as part of the name of the proprietors. I considered that this was wrong marketing policy. We were not allowed to use the words 'Fruit Salt' in the U.S.A. because it was held that the fact that tartaric acid, one of the main ingredients of Eno's, was produced from grapes, was not sufficient justification. I could see the same thing happening in Canada and elsewhere. Anyway, we had already lost the Fruit Salt trade mark in some parts of South America where many people were selling 'Sal de Fruta'. To my mind, 'Eno' was a far more valuable trade mark and I thought that we would eventually have to choose one or the other. I therefore wanted to modernize the pack and use 'Eno' as our trade mark and 'Fruit Salt' as a descriptive term where it was possible. Patten opposed everything and I finally came to the conclusion that he would never accept my leadership. In any event, I wished to start concentrating Group management, so in April 1953 Patten was dismissed and Eno's, Dinneford's Magnesia, and Yeast-Vite were transferred to Macleans whilst Iron Jelloids, Cicfa, Thermogene, and Phosferine went to St Helens.

At the same time control of the overseas business of all companies (outside the Western Hemisphere) was transferred to an Overseas Department overseen by John Rintoul; this eventually became Beecham Overseas Ltd. and by degrees concentrated all our overseas business outside the Western Hemisphere under the ownership and control of one company. As with the home companies we could not achieve this completely until our financial reorganization had been put through, because there were outside Preference shareholders of many of our subsidiary companies, including Eno Proprietaries Ltd. and

Macleans and Brylcreem through their holding company, Beecham Maclean Ltd.

The break up of the Watford Group was the first of those moves that I made to concentrate management into compatible units and to separate overseas from home management. I felt that overseas we should concentrate our efforts on those few brands which were distinctive and capable of massive worldwide development.

10 *Soft Drinks and Beecham Foods*

Lucozade and Coca-Cola

The Group was led into the soft drink business by Lucozade. This great product purchased in 1938 for £90,000 underwrote my early years as Chief Executive of the Group and in its peak year in 1958–59 yielded a profit of £1,500,000. On taking up my appointment in 1951 I believed that with Brylcreem, Macleans Tooth Paste, and Eno's, it could form the basis of a worldwide business. I used to assert that no other company in the world had four such distinctive products. It was my ambition with these brands to build a business in the U.S.A. as large as our business in the U.K. If we could do this the rest of the world would be easy! Meanwhile there was the question of how to develop our Lucozade business in the U.K. and this led us to look very hard at the soft drink market.

We did not know so much about the economics of soft drinks as we do today, but we knew enough to appreciate that volume was needed before it was possible to have a national business at a reasonable selling price. Costs of distribution were such that to deliver much beyond a twenty-five-mile radius of a depot and to truck from factory to depot over distances of much more than fifty miles would force relatively high selling prices. This was the Lucozade problem and during all my period of management of both Macleans and Beechams I was searching for ways and means of reducing Lucozade costs.

I knew that Coca-Cola had started in the U.S.A. as a 'pick-me-up' sold by drug stores and I was always asking myself whether Lucozade could take a somewhat similar route. It is curious that only in Eire has this come about. Therefore, when in 1951 Simon Coombe of Watney Mann Ltd., the brewers, got in touch with me to enquire whether we were interested in joining them to bottle Coca-Cola in the U.K., I responded immediately. Mike Spry, then managing the grocery businesses, was in addition appointed to head our end, and we entered into complex two-way negotiations with Watneys and Coca-Cola.

Coca-Cola had built their worldwide business by means of local bottling franchises. They presented us with their standard agreement which put most of the power in their hands. Watneys and ourselves were both loath to sign this agreement and we argued strongly but to little avail. Our final agreements with Coca-Cola still left them with the power, but they have never used it unreasonably, although in the early days it often took us much longer to get what we wanted than we would have liked.

Subsequently it became apparent that Watneys and Beechams would not always see eye to eye and I went to see Simon Coombe and suggested that instead of maintaining a joint operation covering the whole of England and Wales (with some small exceptions) they took the south and we had the north. This in one sense made a present to Watneys because Coca-Cola had been marketed in the south for a long time, whereas in the north it was being built from scratch. However, I knew that the consumption of soft drinks *per capita* was higher in the north and I thought that this evened things up, giving Watneys the immediate advantage and ourselves the ultimate benefit.

Coca-Cola turned out to be an extremely expensive product to develop in the north of England and for many years we lost money. We were faced with the distribution problem which meant that costs were unreasonably high so long as sales were small. I was also responsible for a big mistake in marketing policy, arguing for a reasonable discount to retailers and a heavy advertising campaign. This proved to be wrong because the retailers, and particularly the dance halls, cafés, and the like, where soft drinks were consumed on the premises, had too much power and could decide to stock only those drinks which yielded them a high profit. I am sure that we would have done better to have given them special discounts at the expense of advertising and to have left the ultimate sellers to make their own prices to the public. Not until comparatively recent times have Beechams made adequate profit from Coca-Cola, helped by the administrative skills of Jim Sullivan, to whom I shall refer elsewhere.

The more we saw of the soft drink market the more it became apparent that the whole business needed rationalization. So far as Beechams were concerned, I felt that we either had to be big, or get out into some other area. If we got out, what would happen to Lucozade? There was the vision of a soft drink business with bottling factories capable of multi-product bottling, strategically placed throughout Great Britain and surrounded by their own depots. If we could ever get to this position I felt that we would be able to dominate the market and be assured of growth for many years. Mike Spry did some exercises which encouraged us. We looked at possible acquisitions and then suddenly in December 1954 there was a big development.

Ribena

In 1947 Sir Brian Mountain had told me that Frank Armstrong, the Chairman, Chief Executive of, and major shareholder in H. W. Carter & Co. Ltd. of Coleford, near Bristol, had approached him at Eagle Star for a loan additional to one already outstanding. Carters was clearly over-trading and had invested, and was continuing to invest, large sums of money in building and equipping its new Coleford factory to an extent unsupportable by its profits, which were low. Sir Brian said that Eagle Star were not happy about the position and he had suggested that Frank Armstrong should see me and discuss a possible sale to Beechams.

I went up to see Frank at Coleford, accompanied by Mac and Ernst Koch, and we were very impressed by the technical excellence of what we saw. I was also impressed by their principal product, Ribena. Before the war Dr Vernon Charley, a scientist employed at Long Ashton Agricultural Research Station, had collaborated with Frank to produce fruit syrups and out of this work emerged Ribena with its very high Vitamin

C content. When war broke out Frank was asked to turn his whole factory over to producing concentrated blackcurrant juice, and he agreed subject to Dr Charley being lent to him for the duration. Other manufacturers were also instructed in the process and blackcurrant juice was reserved for sale to children and invalids.

After the war Frank invited Charley to join him at Carters and they proceeded to build the Coleford factory and greatly expand the plant. They also established laboratories and undertook work which resulted in continuous improvement to the process. They made ten-year contracts with farmers to grow blackcurrants and installed an extensive range of refrigerated storage tanks to store the blackcurrant juice. Sales were very good, and rising, but profit was negligible. It was the same old story – distribution costs could not be brought down to a reasonable level until sales had reached very substantial figures. Added to this, blackcurrants had to be harvested in June and July, the juice immediately expressed and put into the refrigerated storage tanks and subsequently bottled through the remaining ten months. This was a very expensive business.

The company could have been acquired for a relatively small sum of money (I forget how much) and I felt we ought to snap it up. Then I made my big mistake. I concluded that Carters was nearer to Mortons than to Macleans (they had some grocery items) and I recommended to the Beecham Board that it should be acquired for Mortons. Buckley sent Mike Spry up to investigate and he put in a negative report and expressed the view that as the country got back to normal the demand for Ribena would fall away. Buckley then had an interview with Frank, criticized his business, and left him thoroughly upset. Of course, after that, all negotiations for purchase ceased.

When I became Chief Executive in 1951 I asked Frank Armstrong to lunch. He had weathered the worst of his financial troubles with the help of Sir Brian and he was still seething about Buckley, whilst Mike was not exactly his favourite accountant. I pointed out that Buckley had departed and finally he agreed to talk to me if he ever wanted to sell the business. We had lunch from time to time discussing mainly marketing problems and the way his business was developing. Then in December 1954, out of the blue, came the announcement of a proposed sale of Carters to Reckitt & Colman. I was very upset and telephoned Frank who agreed to lunch with me next day. He was apologetic at not getting in touch with me but said that what was proposed was not really a 'take-over' but a 'merger' and he had concluded that the deal with Reckitt & Colman was more in the interests of the company and its staff than a sale to Beechams. I said to him, 'What about your shareholders?' His reply was, 'Damn the shareholders – they are getting a good deal and more than they deserve'. Thereupon I told him that I would demonstrate to him that he could not treat shareholders like that, and we parted.

The next day I called an emergency Board Meeting and obtained its approval to make an improved offer for the Carter business, which I immediately committed to writing, and had delivered to Frank. He came on the telephone in great consternation and I had to tell him that unless he could persuade Reckitt & Colman to meet our offer he would have no alternative but to recommend it to his shareholders. It is clear that his lawyers agreed, because Reckitt & Colman never came back with a better offer, and in due course Frank accepted our offer for himself and his family and he and his Board recommended the offer to the Carter shareholders. The acquisition of Carters enabled us to integrate Lucozade, Ribena, and the Quosh range of squashes into Beecham Foods Ltd. and thus take the first step towards the soft drink business of my dreams. Reckitt & Colman are a fine company but I doubt if Frank's staff would have done better there than with Beechams.

Grocery selling

The growing importance of the grocer as a retailer of an increasing range of proprietary products had been giving us all much to think about for some time. In October 1950 Macleans had set up a grocery sales force selling principally Tooth Paste, Lucozade, Fynnon Salt, and Eno's. When I became Managing Director of Beechams we continued to debate the

14. Though Beecham's Powders were a good remedy for several conditions, earlier advertising tried to cover too many fields. Here the target was 'rheumatic pain' (*ad. dated* June 1951).

15. 'Headache' was the problem here (June 1951) . . .

BEECHAM'S POWDERS are wonderful for COLDS and CHILLS. Owing to their *powder* form they *set to work without delay to bring you speedy, safe relief.* The headachy feeling goes, sneezing stops, uncomfortable shivers and aches subside. Soon you can cheerfully exclaim "Ah! *That's* BETTER!" Be prepared! Carry some Beecham's Powders with you wherever you go and take one *immediately* you feel the first symptoms of Cold or Chill.

Beecham's Powders are also splendid for **INFLUENZA, FEVERISHNESS, HEADACHES, NEURALGIA, RHEUMATIC PAINS** and **NERVE PAINS.** Keep a supply always handy.

2 Powders for 5½d.   Cartons of 8 Powders—1 8d.

16. . . . and 'Colds and Chills' here (December 1951).

It's easy to catch a
SUMMER COLD

Keep BEECHAM'S POWDERS handy!

Standing about after a strenuous game can so easily give you a cold — with sneezing and running eyes — or a feverish chill with muscular aches and pains.

But you'll find that a Beecham's Powder, thanks to its unique formula, will soon have the worst symptoms under control. The fact that Beecham's Powders are in fine powder form makes them easy to assimilate and very speedy in action. Get a supply now. Keep them handy!

2 Powders for 5½d.   Cartons of 8 Powders 1/7

For SUMMER COLDS FEVERISHNESS RHEUMATIC PAINS HEADACHES & NEURALGIA

Take BEECHAM'S POWDERS For QUICK RELIEF!

ALSO AVAILABLE IN TABLET FORM 1/7 PER BOTTLE

17. Eventually Beecham's Powders were advertised for 'colds' alone (*ad. dated* July 1954).

DON'T PUT UP WITH
NEURITIS

AND OTHER NERVE PAINS

Phensic brings quick safe relief!

Don't let pain keep you in misery. Get relief NOW with PHENSIC. Stop the wearying, persistent aching or throbbing.

RELIEVES PAIN

The therapeutic ingredients of PHENSIC act swiftly on nerve centres, bringing quick, safe relief from muscular and nerve pains.

SOOTHES NERVES

PHENSIC tablets soothe strained or overtired nerves, so that you can sleep soundly at night and awake refreshed.

COUNTERACTS DEPRESSION

PHENSIC tablets contain Caffeine as a counter-depressant which counteracts depression. They don't harm the heart or upset the stomach.

Keep a supply of PHENSIC tablets by you. **1/8 & 4/-**. Also in handy envelope pack **4d.**

Phensic

THE SAFE WAY

to relieve **RHEUMATIC PAINS, MUSCULAR PAIN, NERVE PAINS, HEADACHES AND SUMMER COLDS AND CHILLS.**

18. Early Phensic advertising (March 1951).

NEW LIGHT ON HEADACHE

Lifting the "Pain Threshold"

Why aspirin *plus* phenacetin works better than aspirin alone

STEADILY, our knowledge of pain—its cause and its cure—increases with the advance of science.

Researchers have not only charted the *sources* of pain. They have even learned how to *measure* pain.

They have a name for the *lowest degree of pain stimulus that will cause a man or woman to feel pain.* They call it the "pain threshold." And they know which drugs can "lift" the pain threshold—that is, make the patient less sensitive to pain—and by how much, and for how long.

A remarkable combination

Among their greatest discoveries, in the search for a harmless, non-habit-forming drug that would relieve pain, was *aspirin*. Another was *phenacetin* (pronounced fe-nassy-tin).

Perhaps even more remarkable—they have discovered that these two taken together in balanced proportions work better than either aspirin or phenacetin taken alone. And they relieve pain longer.

That is the story behind the Phensic formula. Phensic contains *both* aspirin and phenacetin. This combination goes into action as soon as you take a tablet. Almost at once your headache goes. Moreover, your *emotional reaction* to pain is calmed. And because the Phensic formula also contains caffeine, it counteracts depression.

Fast, effective, long-lasting

What a boon Phensic is to all who suffer from headaches and other kinds of pain! Scientists have found that this formula brings quick and lasting relief wherever the seat of the pain may be. Headaches, nerve pains, toothache, pain from neuralgia, rheumatic conditions, lumbago all yield to the Phensic formula.

Always carry Phensic with you. Then you need never fear an attack of headache wherever you may be!

The PHENSIC *Formula*

Effective and Fast

Does not upset the stomach or harm the heart

IN BOTTLES 1/8 & 4/-. ALSO CONVENIENT 4d. ENVELOPES

19. New-style Phensic advertisement (April 1953), with concentration on its action against 'headache'.

THIS IS A TRUE STORY *about* **Ribena**

"It certainly gets my vote"

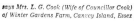

says Mrs. L. G. Cook (Wife of Councillor Cook) of Winter Gardens Farm, Canvey Island, Essex

OPERATION!
In 1948 I was seriously ill and had to undergo a major operation. During my convalescence I drank **Ribena** and made a speedy recovery.

NEW VOCATION!
Fit again when I married in 1952, I was able to cope with the varied tasks of a farmer's wife. This I attributed largely to **Ribena**.

DETERMINATION!
Last year my son was born and I was again taken ill. I arrived home from hospital feeling extremely weak and turned again to **Ribena**.

GRAND SENSATION!
Both my son and I now enjoy **Ribena** regularly. My friends are always telling us how healthy we look. I wouldn't be without it.

Ribena

The Blackcurrant Juice Vitamin 'C' Health Drink
Fights Fatigue and keeps the family fit!

Ribena contains as much as 45% actual blackcurrant juice, one of the richest sources of natural vitamin C, with natural glucose and fruit sugar, sweetened with cane sugar.

ECONOMICAL—Each bottle diluted makes 10 glasses ready to drink.
From your Chemist, Store or Grocer,

DAR5576

20. Ribena strip-cartoon advertisement (March 1955).

21. The strip-cartoon adapted for Lucozade (*test launch*, December 1956).

problem. The break-up of the Watford Group enabled us to streamline our selling to chemists and in July 1953 we formed Harold F. Ritchie Ltd. as group selling agents to grocers. We named this new company Harold F. Ritchie Ltd. as it was to perform exactly the same function as our Canadian sales company of the same name. It took over the Macleans grocery sales force and was accommodated at the Macleans offices on the Great West Road. The Macleans grocery sales for the year to March 1953 were £532,000. Ritchie was aiming at £2·3 million for 1953–54 rising to £3 million for 1955–56. By this time it was planned to have a sales force of 128 men with a six weeks' journey cycle calling on 72,000 out of a total of roughly 130,000 outlets.

I thought that a sales agency company was not the long-term answer to our problems. It separated marketing and selling and there was bound to be friction between the agents and the various companies responsible for marketing and profit. The acquisition of Carters gave us more products capable of being sold to grocers, and I felt that we were now able to take the plunge and set up a big grocery-oriented company.

Beecham Foods

For some time I had been bothered about our top management. I thought it was too weak to sustain rapid growth, particularly growth fed by acquisition of poorly run businesses. Just prior to the acquisition of Carters I had been negotiating with Ralph Hart to join Beechams. He was the European (including the U.K.) Vice-President of Colgate and I had a very high regard for him. At the last minute he was offered the job of Executive Vice-President of Colgate in the U.S.A. and as a result he backed off. Dr Ed Lloyd, the Managing Director of A. C. Nielsen Co. Ltd. in England, advised me to talk to Craig Wood, the Managing Director of Thomas Hedley Ltd., the British subsidiary of Procter & Gamble of the U.S.A. I was given to understand that Craig was unhappy because he no longer had direct access to Mr Neil McElroy, then the Chief Executive of Procter & Gamble, and was more and more being subjected to interference from the newly created overseas division. I saw him, was impressed by him, and in September 1954 he joined Beechams and was appointed to the Board.

I then asked Craig Wood to prepare a plan for the merging of Lucozade, Carters (Ribena and Quosh), Mortons, and the Harold F. Ritchie sales agency into Beecham Foods Ltd. We debated the name and decided that Foods was better than Soft Drinks because Lucozade and Ribena could more accurately be described as 'health' drinks and anyway our main customer would be the grocer.

First of all, we had to find adequate premises from which to operate. Our Headquarters at 68 Pall Mall were small and overfull. There were overflow offices in different parts of London and none of our premises on the Great West Road had any spare space either for new offices or a new warehouse.

B.O.A.C. had moved to London Airport and their old building on the Great West Road had been for sale for some time. County Laboratories had looked at it and turned it down. They were interested in utilizing a large part of the building as a factory (as it had been before the war), but they came to the conclusion that the space capable of being converted to efficient factory operation would be too small. Craig Wood, however, came to me and pointed out that if Headquarters, with its satellite offices also moved to the Great West Road, we could use the major portion of the B.O.A.C. building for offices (Headquarters and Beecham Foods), that we would have ample room for a major depot for our grocery operation, some factory space, and spare land to look after expansion for many years to come. Moreover, we would be able to concentrate Beecham operations in an area where we were already well established. This made sense to me and I authorized him to go ahead.

B.O.A.C. had reduced its price to a very reasonable figure, but by the time we re-appeared on the scene, they had given an option to Felix Fenston, a very astute property man. He refused to sell to us outright, but offered us a 75-year lease of the land (8½ acres) and buildings for £70,000 per annum. Our calculations were that a reasonable market rental was about £60,000. By this time we were all enthusiastic about the site and so I said 'very well offer him £70,000 per annum for a 150-year lease and at the current rate of inflation, by the time it runs out we shall be paying the rent out of petty cash!' Fenston immediately accepted and we obtained the Board's approval to the deal. We named the main building Beecham House and spent a small fortune putting it in first-class order.

Then one day at a cocktail party Fenston boasted to Kenneth Keith that he had made £750,000 on the sale of Beecham House! We were never very sure as to how he arrived at this figure but I believe that his option from B.O.A.C. was at a price of around £560,000. We know that having exercised this option he arranged for a 150-year lease of the site to one of his property companies at a rental of £27,500 per annum, and then sold the freehold to the Church Commissioners, subject to this lease, for £560,000. This gave the Church Commissioners a yield of almost 5 per cent. The property company then gave Beechams a sub-lease for £70,000 per annum and this left Fenston with a profit of £42,500 per annum for 150 years! No doubt by some means or another he could have made £750,000 out of this.

No one likes to be made a fool of and Kenneth was furious with me. I wasn't too happy either and whilst I argued at the time that the principal reason for Fenston's huge profit was the low B.O.A.C. option, I had undoubtedly helped him pile it on by agreeing to pay a high rent and by imagining that taking a very long lease would cure everything. Maybe it would, eventually, for us, but it undoubtedly gave Fenston more. We treated property men with extreme care thereafter!

In spite of everything, we have never regretted the move. We built additional office and laboratory space, gradually transferred all management functions to the site and finally rationalized, and concentrated there, control of all the Group's operations. In due course we bought the freehold for £550,000 and the head lease for £382,500 and I am sure that the current market value is far in excess of this even when the cost of all our additions have been added on.

Craig was an expert on grocery selling and in due course a number of his old associates at Hedleys joined him. When his plan was presented it was very ambitious and based on a monthly call on all grocers. This called for a very large sales force which could not be sustained profitably without an immediate large increase in sales. I should have rejected the plan but I was fascinated by its boldness and half convinced that he could bring it off. His whole team was full of confidence and 'raring to go'.

Then I compounded the error. Craig came to me as the plan began to unfold, said that things were more complex than he had thought, and suggested that the timetable for the change-over be extended. All the overheads had been increased and I knew that delay in implementation would seriously affect the profits for the year and so I demurred and we decided to stick to the original timetable.

The great day came and on 1 April 1955 the four accounting systems were amalgamated and one sales ledger set up on the Morton Powers-Samas punched card system. Orders came pouring in from the sales force and the figures looked good. What we at Headquarters did not appreciate was that travellers had been authorized to take direct orders for as little as £2 in value and a mass of small orders were flooding the accounts department and the delivery system.

In due course I began to get complaints that customers' orders were not being executed and that they could not make sense of their accounts. By this time Mike Spry had joined us at Headquarters as Financial Director and I asked him to go down and enquire into things. Unfortunately, he merely took the Secretary of Beecham Foods (who had formerly been the Morton Financial Director) out to lunch and was assured that apart from teething troubles everything was going well. Then matters got worse and I could no longer ignore information coming from outside. I went down to Brentford with John and Mike and walked round the accounts department. It was obvious that they were in deep trouble and that I had a crisis on my hands of major proportions. The main trouble stemmed from inefficient sales accounting brought about when the four separate systems were combined. Customer numbers were duplicated and many of the month-end customer statements were wrong, either containing too many items or not enough! Total of debtors shot up and we were clearly faced with many months' work to get things right.

The accounting crisis, however, was not the only thing that troubled me. I was disturbed by Craig Wood and his entourage of marketing men whose philosophy was so different from ours. I thought that they were producing over-optimistic budgets involving lavish marketing expenditure, which would not produce the required results.

Another thing that worried me was the advertising. Advertising budgets were well up but in those days we did not have a separate accounting item for 'marketing expenditure'. This was a sub-total in 'advertising' and up to that time it had been quite small. In the case of Ribena and Lucozade practically all money appropriated had been spent on direct advertising. Now substantial expenditures were being planned for 'stunts' and 'deals'.

I remember particularly a competition built around 'Ribena Red' which was intended to popularize a red colour similar to Ribena. This was all very well for soaps and detergents but, in my opinion, fatal for products like Ribena and Lucozade. Then just before the accounting trouble broke Craig had been to see me. He had commissioned some consumer research comparing Lucozade and a competitive product called Ferguzade and this showed a preference for the latter in the ratio, I think, of something like 70–30. As a result he wanted permission to change the Lucozade formula by making it sweeter. I refused and pointed out to him that firstly he would have to carry out long-term research before he could get an accurate answer – short term, the sweeter product nearly always got the bigger preferences. Anyway, we should probably have needed to add sugar if we were to make an acceptable sweeter product and our whole case for Lucozade rested on the superiority of glucose over sugar.

I became convinced that Craig and his boys were too wedded to soap-oriented marketing and that they would fail with our medicinal products, particularly Ribena and Lucozade. No doubt I possessed all the prejudice of the 'medicine man'. I always put my faith in advertising and in the unique product and claim; I was very slow to appreciate the value of consumer and trade deals. After some soul searching I therefore saw Craig and said that in view of the need to reorganize Beecham Foods I was going to transfer him to Headquarters as Marketing Director and appoint John Rintoul Managing Director of Beecham Foods. Craig then went on three months' leave of absence and in due course resigned.

Craig Wood was a director of Beecham Group and I had to know that I retained the Board's confidence. This was the first real test of Kenneth Keith's promise to support me. Just before the Beecham Foods affair broke, we raised £2·38 million by means of a 1 for 8 Rights Issue. Philip Hill had made the issue and I am sure that a lot of institutions had taken up the shares on Kenneth's recommendation. Then when our troubles at Foods became known, the market went sour on us. It says a lot for Kenneth that in the face of his own embarrassment and my débâcle at Beecham Foods, he kept his word to me and continued to back me.

Most of Craig's associates decided to follow him to pastures new and this was my last attempt to improve our top management by going outside. From that day we concentrated on improving the standard of our young recruits, and restricted our intake of outsiders to middle management.

John Rintoul revelled in the job of bringing order out of confusion at Beecham House. He gathered about him a group of able accountants (including Bill Petley, our future Financial Director) and gradually the sales ledgers were put in order and debts collected. Nevertheless, overheads were still running high, sales were poor, and naturally morale was low. The Group profits for the year to March 1956 fell to £3,665,000 from the £3,861,000 of the previous year, and confidence in Beechams, never very strong in those days, declined. The next year did not start well. I had also moved Headquarters to Beecham House and had appointed myself the temporary Marketing Director of Beecham Foods, so as to get the advertising of Lucozade back on course. This was the one product that could revive everything. Its sales had been going ahead strongly until the trouble at Beecham Foods but now the sales were falling, in spite of increased distribution to grocers.

Towards the end of 1956 Frank Armstrong came to me and asked if I would right what he considered a serious injustice. Dorlands had been the advertising agents for Ribena for many years. They had commenced a new campaign consisting of strip cartoons somewhat like small Horlicks advertisements and Frank brought me evidence of their success. Then Craig Wood had sacked them and appointed J. Walter Thompson who had, of course, changed the advertising. Frank felt very strongly that I should hand the account back to Dorlands but I was not prepared to make Beechams look ridiculous. Anyway, there had been successive poor crops of blackcurrants and it looked as if we were going to be unable to produce all the Ribena we could sell so why go to the trouble of changing the advertising again? However, I took the Ribena strip cartoon copy to Royds, who advertised Lucozade, and asked them to adapt the copy to Lucozade and test it. The photographic illustrations show one of the original Ribena advertisements and one of the Lucozade adaptations. We agreed that the best area would be Northern Ireland, which was isolated and had its own depot. The result (towards the end of 1956) was astonishing and we very quickly 'went national' in March the next year. Overleaf is a graph of the Lucozade factory sales before and after the change of advertising.

The effect of this on Beecham Foods was magical. Increased Lucozade sales yielded a high profit. As I have already indicated, increasing volume caused a marked fall in the unit cost of bottling and distribution, and the sudden large increase in sales meant that profits jumped much more than proportionately. This revived the spirits of the Beecham Foods executive and again everything seemed possible. It also had a tremendous effect on Beecham Group: its profits bounded to £4,516,000 in 1957 and to £6,093,000 in 1958 (not all due to Beecham Foods).

I ought to make it clear that the 'strip cartoon' advertising for Lucozade did not remain effective for more than two or three years. It was particularly difficult to relate cause and effect in those days. The jump in sales following strip cartoon

LUCOZADE SALES
Quarterly moving average

advertising was obvious, but we had by then moved into television also. Increasing sales of Lucozade called for the expenditure of much more money in advertising. We had a very adequate press campaign and we spent most of this increase on television. However, in those early days we were never able to measure the effect of this on Lucozade sales and there was some evidence from areas unaffected by commercial television that it was negligible. Our television commercials for Lucozade never seemed to me to be believable until those produced by the London Press Exchange Ltd. when we moved the account to them in June 1960.

Nevertheless, nothing we did was able to prevent the gradual decline of Lucozade sales to the rate prevailing before we resorted to the strip cartoon advertising. I am glad to say that since I retired growth has begun again, based on the London Press Exchange television copy. This is addressed to mothers and sells Lucozade for children who are ill, or recovering from illness, and reminds the mother that she also can get a 'lift' from taking a drink. I have enormous faith in Lucozade and believe that work carried out first by Ernst Chain whilst he was in Rome, and subsequently by Beecham scientists, has established the superiority of glucose over sugar. I personally keep my consumption of sugar to a minimum but drink Lucozade freely, believing that it provides immediate energy without increasing blood cholesterol and body fat. I regard it as an alternative to alcohol for giving one a 'lift' and believe that, in spite of its success in Geat Britain and Eire, it is still a 'sleeper' in the Beecham stable and capable of worldwide development.

The success of Lucozade in 1956–57 did not solve our problems. We still had not achieved our ambition in actually reducing total overheads and clearly the size and complexity of Beecham Foods was presenting us with problems. Jack Smartt was Factory Director and Jim Sullivan was responsible to him for the distribution system and for the food and confectionery factories. These were the areas chiefly responsible for our high overheads. Some factories, particularly Lowestoft, were seriously under-employed and long delivery runs both to depots from factories and to customers from factories and depots were keeping costs high. Jim commenced his long hard battle to bring about improvement and we were fortunate to have a man of such outstanding administrative ability available.

Thomas & Evans

In 1958 Frank Armstrong introduced me to Mr W. D. James, the Chairman of Thomas & Evans Ltd. of Porth, Glamorgan. This company had started as a small soft-drink bottling business and had grown very substantially in Wales and the South and Midlands. It sold 26-ounce bottles of soft drinks very largely from door to door, employing a substantial staff of vanmen operating over 1,000 lorries and delivering soft drinks out of its bottling factories and depots to approximately 1 million households.

Mr James, who was then over 70 years of age, was anxious to sell and his senior colleague on the Board supported him. However, they believed that the two junior members of the Board, who carried out most of the executive duties, would be opposed to the sale and Mr James was anxious to agree the terms to be placed before his Board before the two younger members were involved. We agreed terms after some argument and later I was informed that these had been approved by the Board of Thomas & Evans for recommendation to its shareholders. However, there was bitter antagonism from one of the young directors who got in touch with Sir Frederic Hooper, Chairman of Schweppes and, in due course, Schweppes made a counter-bid. Then transpired the worst bid battle I was ever involved in.

Schweppes's action revealed their concern at Beechams invasion of the soft drinks business and we took it as a sign that they were trying to keep us out. This confirmed us in our desire to get in. I was particularly interested in the Thomas & Evans door-to-door business. It seemed to me that this presented us with a wonderful opportunity to try out new drinks and hopefully to develop a new national brand. In addition there was Lucozade. If we could add this product to the Thomas & Evans range sold off their vans, how much could they sell? Even a few bottles per van per day would make an enormous difference to the sales. In the event, we never succeeded in developing a new national brand and our trials of selling Lucozade from the vans were a failure, but it was these ambitions that encouraged us to top the bids made by Schweppes. Our final offer, which made Schweppes withdraw, valued Thomas & Evans at £7·65 million and the lucky shareholders snapped it up.

It is debatable whether we were justified in paying such a high price for Thomas & Evans. Considered in isolation it certainly was not worth the money but, on the other hand, I thought then, and still believe, that we were right to pursue the ambition to establish Beecham as a major factor in the soft drink business. We tried many ideas in Thomas & Evans and other acquisitions have now been merged into it. Up to the time of my retirement it could not be said that we had achieved all our objectives but the last word has not been written. We had gone a long way to rationalizing the Group soft drink business, thanks very largely to Jim Sullivan who controlled it during the vital years; maybe one day Beechams will realize that dream of mine and possess multiple-product filling lines, strategically situated with their satellite depots throughout the land.

Development of Grocery Sales

The acquisition of Thomas & Evans made no immediate contribution to solving the Beecham Foods problems and we were clearly faced with a long period of steady rationalization. This had to proceed in conjunction with strong marketing policies directed not only to increasing sales wherever possible but particularly to increasing sales in those areas where only greater turnover could overcome our factory overhead problem.

This was the case with Morton canned vegetables. We had a substantial sale of canned garden peas, but these were harvested in June and July and the pack was completed early in August. Morton's canning factory at Lowestoft was therefore very busy for about three months and then was seriously under-employed. We needed products that could be canned throughout the year. Runner beans, broad beans, and carrots, which ripened at other times of the year, helped. So did growing early and late varieties of peas but we could not solve the problem until we had developed the sale of a wide variety of canned products including processed peas (i.e. dried peas reconstituted).

Again, we were faced with the problem of size and we considered selling the canning business and the Morton brand. This was probably our best policy and had we, during the period 1956–58, found a suitable buyer to whom we could have entrusted the staff, we could well have sold out. We were proud of our conditions of service which we thought better than most. Furthermore, Lowestoft was an area of high unemployment and we felt that the factory staff, amongst the most loyal in the Group, would be subjected to a double risk unless we could sell the business to people of integrity. In the event, we soldiered on and in 1959 all question of selling out was finally rejected. Here is an extract from our Group Management Committee minutes of 12 May 1959:

> The Chairman said that the future of the Lowestoft factory required further consideration.
>
> Lowestoft was essentially a canning factory and there was nothing to be gained in the long term by subsidising its economy by means of sweet production as this would only militate against the proper development of the Confectionery Division. It had already been decided that the Group's responsibility as employers in Lowestoft prohibited any plans to close down or sell the factory. It followed that there would have to be development in canning which would ensure the efficient and profitable operation of the factory.
>
> It was agreed that consideration be given to utilising the entire capacity of the factory in producing high quality products to sell, if necessary at a premium price and to include the following:
>
> > Garden Peas
> > Runner Beans
> > Broad Beans
> > Carrots
>
> Processed Peas will be produced when the above products are out of season.

The basic idea behind Beecham Foods was to build up an organization which could market our products to the grocer as strongly and as efficiently as the big 'soapers', Unilever, Procter & Gamble, and Colgate. We were particularly concerned to match Unilever who covered the whole country with a distribution system having depots strategically placed so as to reduce cost to a minimum and at the same time achieve maximum speed of delivery. This, of course, rested on the fact that they were selling thousands of tons of soaps, detergents, and canned goods. We wanted also to build up tonnage, and this was one of the arguments in favour of attempting to build up Mortons into a substantial canning business.

Lucozade, Ribena and then the Quosh range of squashes helped. One of the reasons for attempting to build a confectionery business rested on the possibility of combining distribution but the plain fact was that we could not match Unilever unless we competed with them head-on in soaps or detergents or canned goods on a massive scale. In the event we did not do too badly. Jim Sullivan worked away at the distribution system and when in 1966 we finally put everything together under the Products (U.K.) Division, we operated very efficiently for our size and we did not think that we were at too serious a disadvantage compared with our competitors.

To show what a revolution had taken place in retailing and the problems we faced, here is a Nielsen Market Research breakdown of Group sales by type of outlet in the year to March 1951, compared with the year to March 1970:

	Sales through Grocers %	Sales through Chemists %
1951	39·0	61·0
1970	77·6	22·4

11 *Western Hemisphere*

Following my appointment as Managing Director I turned with high hopes to deal with what we called the 'Western Hemisphere'. This was the U.S.A., Canada, and the countries of South America.

The Group's business there flowed from the acquisition of Eno Proprietaries Ltd. in 1938. This was one of Philip Hill's most fateful purchases, giving the Group the nucleus of its future international business by providing companies around the world – including those in Canada, the U.S.A., and South America – on which we could base our efforts.

The story starts with Harold F. Ritchie Ltd. of Toronto, Canada. Before the last war this was a sales agency business dominated by Harold F. Ritchie himself, a colourful character known as 'car load Ritchie' because of his penchant for seeking orders for car loads of merchandise. Ritchie was Canadian selling agent for many U.S. and British companies including Dole Pineapple, a very big seller, and J. C. Eno. In 1927 through his Canadian company he bought the business of J. C. Eno Ltd. throughout the world and also a controlling interest in the business of Scott & Bowne Inc. in the U.S.A., which owned the Western Hemisphere rights to Scott's Emulsion. Then Ritchie died suddenly and British interests acquired Harold F. Ritchie Ltd. of Canada and in 1934 floated Eno Proprietaries Ltd. in the U.K. as the holding company of all the Eno companies around the world, of the Scott's Emulsion business in the Western Hemisphere, and of Harold F. Ritchie Ltd. of Canada.

So as to produce impressive figures for the prospectus issued on the London market, Eno's 'Fruit Salt' was offered to the trade in the U.S.A. and Canada with very attractive 'deals', and in consequence, high sales and profits were shown in the six months to 30 June 1934. But, of course, in the following period all the merchandise in the hands of the trade had to be sold to the public and factory sales fell. Advertising in the U.S.A. was cut and this caused a further fall in sales (never to be recovered) which in due course brought about a substantial fall in the profits of the parent company, Eno Proprietaries Ltd., and a fall in value of that company's shares on the London Stock Exchange. It was this fall which at that time made shares of companies like Eno unpopular on the Stock Exchange and resulted in 'Mossy' Myers of the stockbroking firm of Myers & Co. advising the Maclean Board against an attempt to follow up its issue of Preference Shares with an offer to the public of the company's Ordinary Shares. Thus, after the breakdown of negotiations with Sterling Drug of U.S.A., Philip Hill seized his chance and bought Macleans. Then, as has been mentioned, in the following year he made a public bid for the Eno Proprietaries shares and acquired that business also.

Harold F. Ritchie had attempted to put over a sharp deal when he acquired control over the majority share interest in Scott & Bowne Inc. By his purchase of stock from the estate of Mr Bowne's widow, he controlled the Board of Scott & Bowne and put through an agreement with his master company, Harold F. Ritchie Ltd. of Canada, appointing that company selling agents for Scott's Emulsion on terms which appropriated most of the profits to Ritchie. At this time, the minority shareholders included the Methodist Church of the U.S.A., both Mr and Mrs Bowne having each left the Church a substantial number of shares at death. The finances of the Methodists had been reorganized and greatly improved by one of their ordained Ministers, Dr Frederick B. Newell. Fred was a very able man and he would have made a fine Bank President. Had he been employed on Wall Street he would probably have made a fortune. When Ritchie made his move, Fred got in touch with the other minority shareholders who all employed as their lawyer Stuart Updike of the law firm of Townley, Updike & Carter. Fred and Stuart then confronted Ritchie and threatened a lawsuit.

After long argument the matter was settled on terms which

included cancelling the contract appointing the selling agency and appointing Fred and Stuart to the Board of Scott & Bowne Inc. for the purpose of looking after the interests of the minority stockholders. They were not going to trust Ritchie any more!

By the time Beecham acquired Scott & Bowne Inc. the minority stockholders had been bought out, but the two non-executive directors remained. This was a piece of luck for Beechams. Both Fred and Stuart were fascinated by 'marketing' which in the U.S.A. was not regarded as an inferior occupation as in the U.K. at that time. Later on Fred became the Methodist Bishop of New York and he used to boast that by applying the marketing lessons learnt during his association with Beechams to his diocese, he had greatly increased its efficiency. Buckley merged Scott & Bowne Inc. with J. C. Eno Inc. and there was a period following his sackings when top management of the new company Eno-Scott & Bowne Inc. was almost non-existent. For a temporary period Stuart held the fort as part-time Chief Executive and following that he and Fred constituted themselves an Executive Committee to oversee and monitor the performance of the Chief Executive. When I took over they were both most helpful to me in acquiring a 'feel' of the American scene and Stuart remained the company's lawyer until the mid-1960s.

Almost as soon as the war ended affairs in the U.S.A. began to assume major importance in Beechams. Stanley Holmes went to New York regularly and a number of us paid visits to both Canada and the U.S.A. The U.S. business did not generate any worthwhile profit but the Canadian business did, and one or two South American companies made money. There were a number of poor attempts to launch Beechams brands in the U.S.A., including Macleans Tooth Paste on the West Coast, but everything was badly done and anyway there simply was not enough money to do a proper job. During the war the Bank of England had insisted on the remittance of all overseas profits to the U.K. and most of our overseas companies were short of cash. It was not possible to refinance those in the dollar area because the Bank would not approve any transference of funds.

Brylcreem had been very successful in Canada, but competition from the U.S.-owned Wildroot cream hairdressing was intensifying and Bob Alexander, the President of the Canadian company, had been warning Stanley Holmes that unless we could launch Brylcreem in the U.S.A. he would be fighting with one arm tied behind his back. The trouble was that U.S. magazine and radio advertising (and later television advertising) flowed over into Canada from the U.S.A. and thus reinforced Canadian advertising for U.S. products. As a result Wildroot was heavily outspending Brylcreem and we were feeling the pinch. It was clear to everybody that we had to make a serious effort in the U.S.A. but there was not much agreement on how to go about it.

In 1947–48 Stanley Holmes was put in touch with Mr Noble, the Chairman and dominant shareholder of Mint Products Inc., makers of Life Savers, a mint sweet with a hole in it. The company had several million dollars of spare cash and Mr Noble was interested in financing the marketing of Brylcreem in the States. The proposition involved the forming of a separate company, jointly held by Beechams and Mint Products, to acquire the rights to Brylcreem in the U.S.A. Mint Products would put up a maximum of $4 million in stages and as required, to finance advertising, inventory, and the like, depending on the success of test-markets. There were endless discussions about this. N. F. Fabricius was very upset and begged me to help him prevent the deal. He believed that we should eventually lose control of our product and he was frightened of any deal with an American, believing that they always expected to be top dog. Anyway, the negotiations bogged down.

As soon as General Buckley became Managing Director, he travelled to New York and addressed himself to the problems. He sacked some of our executives there and put in train a scheme produced by Hobrow which transferred ownership of all the South American companies to our U.S. company. Those South American profits which were classified by the respective Governments as remittable thus arrived in the U.S. and provided some minimal funds for development. He also put together our two Canadian companies. The Eno and Ritchie executives were at loggerheads. Ritchie was selling agent for Eno and it had a warehouse but no factory. J. C. Eno had a factory but no sales force and was therefore merged into Harold F. Ritchie Ltd., so that Bob Alexander became responsible for all our Canadian interests. Both these moves proved very useful.

Sporadic attempts had been made to develop Brylcreem sales in the U.S.A., the last one starting in 1950 and running through into 1951 when I made my first visit as Managing Director. The Beecham U.S. business was being managed by a man brought up in a drug store chain (like Boots but without any manufacturing facilities). Advertising expenditure was scattered about and included posters, radio, and substantial sums on 'co-operative advertising'. This involved paying retail drug or grocery chain stores for mention in their large press advertisements of goods which they stocked and which they then 'featured' in their stores. Our profits were negligible.

The Brylcreem pricing policy appalled me. Our management considered it necessary to be cheaper than the major competition and to give better terms to the trade. Then they were endeavouring to copy the British policy of concentrating a lot of attention on the barber. In the U.S.A. this was impossible except perhaps for a highly priced line. Distribution to barbers had to be effected through the barber jobbers (wholesalers) who demanded very large discounts. I calculated that on all Brylcreem sold through the barber we had 3 per cent of the selling price to cover advertising and profit!

It was clear that what we needed in the Western Hemisphere was management with a large 'M'. This is the usual problem with overseas business and, in my opinion, is the main obstacle every international company has to overcome. My first endeavour was to seek an American partner and I was introduced to Abe Plough of Plough Inc. At that time his business rested very largely on St Joseph's Aspirin for Children. He was a 'medicine man' and a real dynamo, whom I liked, and felt that I could get on with. My proposal was that we merged our two businesses in the Western Hemisphere (at that time he had no business elsewhere) leaving Beechams with 40 per cent and Abe Plough and his family and associates with 60 per cent. Abe was not prepared to allow us to acquire such a large chunk of his business and I finally came down to 25 per cent. However, we could not come to terms and we parted.

Bob Alexander was highly agitated at my endeavours to merge with Plough. I told him frankly that we needed good management in the U.S.A. which at present I considered very poor. He pressed the point that we could find management ability in the Ritchie business in Canada and produced for my inspection Maurice Bale, at that time an Area Sales Manager with Ritchie. Maurice was young, enthusiastic, and clearly a two-fisted fighter and I agreed to abandon my search for a partner and soldier on alone in the U.S.A. We set up Beecham (Canada) Ltd. in Canada to hold and control all our Western Hemisphere business, and Bob Alexander was appointed President of this company and also President of the U.S. business. Maurice Bale was appointed Executive Vice-President in the U.S.A. with a promise that he would be made President if he 'made out'.

We then reviewed our position in the U.S.A. Eno's had continued to decline, following the cuts in advertising, and sales were now static at the rate of little more than $200,000 per annum. We set about testing advertising copy and rates of expenditure capable of building sales. At that time Canadian sales of Eno's were running at the rate of $1 million per annum and if we could achieve half the Canadian *per capita* sales in the U.S.A. we should have a very big business indeed. This was a very tempting prospect but we were up against formidable opposition, particularly Alka-Seltzer which, although based on aspirin, was sold for stomach upsets. Many tests were carried out in small areas but none of them, right up to the time of writing this book, has produced figures which justified a major effort.

My immediate interest was Brylcreem. Our experience in Canada had already made it clear that the product would sell – we had to find a way of doing it economically and profitably. In 1951 Brylcreem had scattered distribution throughout the U.S.A., chiefly in some drug store chains and in some hairdressers. This had been increased as a result of the small-scale advertising efforts of the past two years and some food store chains were stocking it. Sales were running at the rate of approximately $500,000 per annum. We had to spend what was left of the year to 31 March 1952 in planning our strategy, increasing prices, improving packaging, and gearing up for increased production in the factory.

There were some tense arguments over the pack. In England, 95 per cent of Brylcreem had always been sold in a glass jar. The U.S. pack, on the other hand, was a tube and N. F. Fabricius argued strongly that we ought to follow the British practice and feature the jar. He also wanted the British advertising to be taken as a model and adapted to U.S. idiom. This advertising was of the masculine type using sportsmen as presenters. Bill Atherton, our U.S. advertising agent (son of a one-time manager of the Beecham's Pills factory in the U.S.A.), was strongly against both the jar and the British advertising. He wanted the tube and 'sex', and his copy was humorous and concentrated on Brylcreem helping the male to get his mate. It also contained the slogan 'a little dab'll do ya' which made Fab see red.

The use of Brylcreem was a religious observance with all at County. They used to scoop great dollops of the cream out of the jar and anoint their hair with it. Fab gave us a demonstration in New York and poured scorn on the 'little dab'. Bill stuck to his guns and was supported by the U.S. Executive. Much to Fab's annoyance and against the principles both he and I believed in (that other things being equal, successful advertising in the U.K. should be used overseas) I let the U.S.A. pursue the tube and sex. I also supported the 'little dab' because I believed that our U.S. claim that Brylcreem was 'not greasy, not messy' was only true if a small quantity was used. I suppose that I was also influenced by my own usage. For some time I had been using the tube so that I could accurately measure out a small quantity every day. Events clearly showed that the Americans were right on all counts.

The profits generated in South America were clearly not going to be sufficient for our needs and so we applied to the Exchange Control Department of the Bank of England for permission to guarantee a loan from the Bank of Montreal in Canada to our U.S. Company of up to $1,250,000. I had already ascertained that they were ready to lend. We had some discussions with representatives of the Bank of England and there was a massive meeting attended by representatives from numerous Government departments. John Rintoul finally produced a masterly letter and supporting memoranda extending in all to fourteen foolscap pages! This gave extensive information about the market and past performance of Brylcreem in other markets. After reading it, I was more confident than ever! Included in the letter was an estimate of sales and profits and losses for the first three years. I thought this rather stupid but we were asked for it and so we pulled some figures 'out of the air'. Here is an extract from John's letter:

	Year	Consumer Sales	Advertising Expenditure	Earned Advertising	Annual Deficit	Cumulative Deficit
	1950	394	216	–	–	–
Est.	1951	492	237	–	–	–
Est.	1952	800	800	280	520	520
Est.	1953	1,200	800	480	320	840
Est.	1954	2,000	800	800	–	–

(U.S. $'000)

Cumulative deficit, say, $850,000

The additional investment in stocks and debtors to finance an additional sales volume of $1,500,000 per annum may be estimated at $350,000 attributable as to $175,000 in respect o stocks and as to $175,000 in respect of debtors.

It may thus be estimated that the full development campaign will call for finance up to $1,250,000 over a three year period to provide for:

		$
(i) Development Advertising		850,000
(ii) Liquid Assets		
(a) Stocks	175,000	
(b) Debtors	175,000	350,000
		1,200,000
	Say	$1,250,000

It is interesting to compare these sales figures with those actually achieved:

		($'000)	
	Projected		Actual
1950–51	394		415
1951–52	492		599
1952–53	800		854
1953–54	1,200		1,012
1954–55	2,000		1,629
1955–56	–		3,370

The Bank of England gave its formal consent and we obtained our line of credit from the Bank of Montreal. Our national radio campaign was launched in April 1952 following a strong effort on the part of an augmented sales force to obtain reasonable distribution. This remained patchy and sales did not excite us. We were spending at the rate of $800,000 per annum on a national campaign, which was much too low anyway.

When I visited New York in November 1952 it was becoming clear that our existing plans would not work. Sales were not good enough and radio advertising was taking a tremendous knock from television. Sets were multiplying at a great rate and Nielsen were recording massive increases in television viewing and a substantial fall-off in listening to radio. I had demanded that we marshal all our resources to spend the maximum on radio but at Bill Atherton's insistence had allowed a small television test. Bill's son, Jack, was a gifted musician whose one wish was to play in an orchestra and to make a living from music. He was not happy in advertising but he could write memorable jingle music. He created the jingle:

> Brylcreem – a little dab'll do ya
> Brylcreem – you look so debonair
> Brylcreem – the girls will all pursue ya
> Simply rub a little in your hair.

The jingle was played in the television commercial shown in the test-market which did not use human actors, but puppets – girls stroking a boy's hair and subsequently chasing him. Results from this test were very good.

We agreed that an immediate switch was called for but we had to take some hard decisions. Even in those days television advertising was expensive. Moreover, in prime time, when the bulk of people were listening, all shows were sponsored mostly for national coverage at costs way above our resources. In addition I wanted our message to reach a minimum number of people frequently. I put this at 20 per cent of potential viewers four times a month. This meant that we could not cover the whole country and would have to concentrate on a region. We also could not use 'prime' time and so we put all our money into late-night 'spot' advertisements. We chose the East and West Central areas of the U.S.A. because we could bring stronger sales pressure to bear there and because it was a heavy hairdressing consumption area which was also close to Canada. The late-night spots did enable us to reach a high proportion of young men although I am sure that we failed to achieve my minimum figures at the start.

The new campaign got underway early in 1953 and we were able to bring much greater sales pressure to bear in the smaller area. Almost immediately it had the smell of success and everyone became enthused. The financial year 1953–54 produced a sale of $1,011,000. Then we moved into the West Coast Area and 1954–55 gave us sales of $1,629,000 with advertising of $1,087,000. In 1955 we moved across to the Eastern seaboard so that we covered the whole of the U.S.A. other than the South. Our sales in 1955–56 reached $3,370,000 with advertising $1,895,000. We went 'national' in 1956 and made our first profit in 1956–57 selling $4,626,000 worth, spending $2,220,000 in advertising, and making $130,000 profit! From then on sales went steadily upwards until they reached $12,543,000 in 1961–62 with $4,062,000 of advertising and a brand profit of $3,391,000. However, this overstates the position for at that time we had launched Silvikrin Shampoo nationally, sharing advertising with Brylcreem, and Silvikrin was losing $1,740,000!

Our appointment of Bill Atherton as advertising agent was terminated on 31 March 1958. This was a hard thing to do, especially in view of his help in the early days. However, Bill's agency was very small and I did not think that he could give us the services we needed when we came to launch tooth paste. We made suitable financial arrangements and I am glad to say that Bill remained my very good friend right up to his death a few years ago.

The big decision was whether we had the muscle to invade the dentifrice market. This had been dominated by Colgate and at that time Procter & Gamble were spending vast sums bludgeoning their way in with Gleem, and then launching Crest, the first fluoride tooth paste. I decided that we had best wait and first of all launch a shampoo.

The shampoo market was nearly as large as the tooth paste market and there was no dominant brand. It seemed to me that provided we could put up a good shampoo, and I thought we had several in England, and provided we did the job properly, we could not fail to gain 3 per cent of the market, which would be worth $3 million and help greatly with our overheads even if we did not make a profit.

Television advertising was becoming more and more expensive. Fortunately, sponsoring of shows was going out and 'spots' could be bought at any time. We had to get into prime time advertising to reach sufficient people but to do this with one-minute commercials meant sacrificing frequency. We therefore had discussions with the A.B.C. network and succeeded in making a deal with them to split a minute of time between two brands. Now I had proved to my satisfaction in England that one could keep advertising running at a high frequency for twelve weeks and then take six weeks' holiday before sales started to suffer. This was done with a medicine (Fynnon Salt) and I was confident that if this pattern worked for that type of product it would work for toiletries. Therefore, if we had three brands we could rotate them so that each was on for twelve weeks and off for six. Of course, this could only be done for the basic expenditure and the brands needing more advertising would have to use supplementary spots. How nice it all is in theory!

My idea was that with Brylcreem, Silvikrin Shampoo, and Macleans Tooth Paste we should have three products and I could see us achieving a total turnover in excess of $50,000,000 and soon the U.S. business would be larger than that in the U.K.! It could have been done, I am sure, but we made too many mistakes and I failed to realize that the American reaction to success of a competitor is much more ruthless than the British.

So we chose to launch Silvikrin Shampoo. It was our most successful shampoo in England but, with hindsight, was not the brand we should have attempted to put on the U.S. market. First of all, the name was peculiar and some people thought it was for grey or silver hair. Then the product was an efficient cleaner but probably not the best for dry hair (there are three different Silvikrin products now for dry, normal, and greasy hair). Yet in the average conditions in the U.S.A. dry hair and dandruff are very prevalent. Finally, we should have tested at least one of our other brands before we took a decision. In the event, our test did not really justify a launch. We were able to manufacture evidence from it that we could achieve 3 per cent of the market and break even, and we were cock-a-hoop over Brylcreem and greatly over-confident. So away we went on what turned out to be a catastrophe.

We launched Silvikrin Shampoo nationally in August 1960, using, in the main, half-minute television commercials 'back to back' with Brylcreem. In 1960–61 we spent $1,506,000 and sold $728,000 which was at least $500,000 less than we should have sold. The next year was vital to us and we gambled heavily on both Brylcreem and Silvikrin with the catastrophic 'record deal'.

Maurice Bale was approached by a man who had previously done business with us with a superficially attractive proposal. This was to supply us with hundreds of thousands of long-playing gramophone records using well-known artists in music 'spectaculars'. We could take these records from his firm at a very low price, this to include a cover suitably printed to support the 'deal'. Then we would give them away first with a tube of Brylcreem and, at a later date, a different record with a bottle of Silvikrin Shampoo. There was a guarantee that unsold records would be taken back for credit. This plan was written up, evaluated, and put before me with a recommendation to go. I was enthusiastic and hoped that it would establish Silvikrin Shampoo on the market. I should have asked John Rintoul to have examined the scheme in detail with the collaboration of Stuart Updike, our lawyer!

First of all the Brylcreem deal seemed to go quite well and we went straight on to Silvikrin. Then the trouble began to show and everyone went to great lengths to keep me from knowing just how bad things were. If only we had called a halt then we could have saved something from the wreck but, as it was, we went on churning out packed stock combined with records that we had no hope of selling.

The salesmen were doing their best. Retailers were accepting large deliveries on a guaranteed sale or return, but the 'deal' was not being bought by the public. We had paid for all stocks of records delivered to us but things had gone wrong at our supplier's end. He was in trouble over copyright with one of the artists used. Then his costs must have been higher than he had calculated because he was not paying all his bills.

Finally, came the reckoning. Vast quantities were being returned to us by the trade and we also had heavy stocks in our warehouses. One of the artists turned on us with a claim and it became very clear that the supplier was quite unable to meet his guarantee. I sent John Rintoul out to investigate and report to the Board and Stuart Updike took over and dealt both with the claims against us – which were numerous but without much merit – and our claim against the supplier. As a result of all this we wrote off $1 million against Brylcreem marketing costs and $500,000 against Silvikrin. This really marked the end of our drive to establish Silvikrin on the U.S. market. Some of the advertising was continued into the next year until Tooth Paste took over, but everyone knew that Silvikrin was finished.

In May 1959, prior to the Silvikrin launch, Bob Alexander retired. This facilitated the transferance of financial and overall management control from Canada to the U.S.A. The U.S. company had developed and was larger than the Canadian.

With Maurice Bale as President of the U.S. company it was much more efficient to give him a competent financial man and to base our overall control of the whole of the Western Hemisphere including South America in the U.S.A. Beecham (Canada) Ltd. was wound up and the ownership of Harold F. Ritchie Ltd. of Canada transferred to Eno-Scott & Bowne Inc. at Clifton, New Jersey. Thus this company owned and controlled all the Beecham companies in the Western Hemisphere. Its name was then changed to Beecham Products Inc. and that of Ritchie Canada to Beecham Products Ltd. Maurice Bale's responsibility for the area of course excluded pharmaceuticals.

Then on 1 January 1962 the first Divisional Organization of Beecham Group was set up. I deal with this in Chapter 13. It is sufficient to say here that this resulted in Maurice Bale and Ed Rose of Canada being transferred to England and in my resigning as Chairman of Beecham Products Inc. for roughly a year. Then when things did not work out we all reverted to our previous jobs. We had a crisis on our hands in the U.S.A. The Silvikrin mess had to be cleared up quickly and we needed to launch Tooth Paste.

These were hectic days because at the same time our new Pharmaceutical Division was putting the first Beecham penicillins on the world market. Doug Stafford was visiting the U.S.A. for endless arguments with Bristol-Myers Co. over our agreement and he was also addressing himself to the problem of putting our own antibiotic brands on the Western Hemisphere markets.

Ronnie Halstead was in the U.S.A. operating as Western Hemisphere manager for the Pharmaceutical Division. His first visit to the States was in 1955 as factory manager for Beecham Products Inc. Whilst holding this job he had off his own bat taken courses in marketing at the New York Management College. Then in 1960 Doug Stafford had called for him to assume the position of Assistant Managing Director of Beecham Research Laboratories Ltd. Under Bob Wilkins he set up the first Beecham Detail Force in England to call on doctors and he did this brilliantly. Following this he had returned to the U.S.A. on behalf of the Pharmaceutical Division with instructions to develop the antibiotic business in the U.S.A., Canada, and South America.

This gives some idea of the stresses and strains at that time. We were overstretched in Beecham Products and soon after Tooth Paste was launched I called on Doug Stafford to release Ronnie Halstead and appointed him Marketing Vice-President of Beecham Products Inc. This probably delayed our development of the pharmaceuticals, particularly in South America, but I felt that I had no choice. The proprietary business had suffered enough from the drain of its finest man-power to Pharmaceuticals and we had to do something to redress the balance. Doug Stafford had been very shrewd in his choice of executive staff. He had taken Bob Wilkins from the U.S.A. and his departure had seriously depleted our management there. The new Pharmaceutical Division was doing very well, but we were clearly suffering in the proprietary business.

The launch of Tooth Paste in the U.S.A. began towards the end of 1962–63. For this we chose the West Coast and divided it into three areas, Los Angeles, San Francisco, and Portland, Oregon. In all these areas we used substantially the same advertising, concentrating our claims on whiter teeth, but there were different weights of spending. I had had a great fight with the advertising agents over this and they had gone as far as they dared in disclaiming responsibility for failure. They were convinced that we had to make stronger claims to be successful and they were also unhappy about my insistence on following closely our Danish Tooth Paste advertising.

I had visited Denmark in 1961 and found a remarkable state of affairs there. The manager of the business was a great character named 'Bobby' Bengsston. He had previously worked for Colgate and tooth paste was in his blood, so to speak. There was no television advertising allowed in Denmark at that time, but he had decided to use cinema advertising *and to produce the films himself.* He rented facilities and using amateur talent produced some magnificent films, using young boys and girls of about 17 years. The theme was young love and white teeth and the setting was a swimming pool, or by the sea, or in snow. I do not think that anyone can be sure what copy will sell goods until it does. When this happens I believed then, and now, that substantially the same copy will sell anywhere in the world where the state of civilization is roughly the same. Bengsston with his copy had captured more than one-third of the Danish tooth paste market, something we have never approached anywhere else.

When for a short time I took over as Chairman of the Toiletry Division I set about persuading our people throughout the world to adopt the Danish copy. This proved to be very difficult both because of the jealousy of overseas executives and the opposition of advertising agents, who could not bring themselves to accept someone else's copy. In England, Norman Moore had retired as Chairman of Bensons and I reluctantly decided that it would be better to bring about a fundamental change in Tooth Paste advertising by transferring the account to the London Press Exchange. They promptly put the actual Danish film on British television, suitably dubbed. It was this copy, magnificently carried on and extended by London Press Exchange, which led to the revival of Macleans Tooth Paste in Britain and, when the U.S.A. had demonstrated what could be done, throughout the world.

But to return to America: in Los Angeles we launched Tooth Paste in conjunction with Brylcreem, banding the two products together and offering them at the price of Brylcreem alone. On the other hand, in San Francisco we used 'sampling', distributing door-to-door a small-sized tube of Macleans Tooth Paste as a free sample with suitable literature. These samples went to one-third of the homes of families above the low income groups. Finally, in Portland we used a large tube as a sample.

It was very quickly apparent that the sampling method was the best. It was very costly but one could extrapolate results and show that, leaving the cost of sampling to be written off separately, Tooth Paste was making a profit in a remarkably short space of time. Macleans' share of the market in the sampled areas as shown by the Nielsen Survey jumped very rapidly to 5 per cent. This nationally at that time was equal to an annual sale of $7,400,000.

Our problem, therefore, was how quickly could we move across the country within our physical and financial resources. The cost of sampling had to be written off in the year in which it was done. We had also to produce the millions of tubes required and pack and dispatch them. It was also vital to 'sell' the trade and support the sampling campaign with displays in the stores. All this fell on Maurice Bale's shoulders but he soon had strong support from Ronnie Halstead and, in my opinion, it was this campaign which completed Ronnie's education as a marketing man.

The early launches had not shown whether the small or the large sample produced the best results. As we rolled across the country we relied mainly on the large sample but we continued to give the small sample in some areas. By the time we reached the centre, however, the position was clear and the large sample proved much superior.

The history of sampling in Beechams is interesting. Small give-away samples were in common usage in many product categories, particularly tooth paste. I think also that some U.S companies had given away the standard small size, when introducing a new product but I do not believe on anything like our scale. Curiously enough, Hunter had used sampling to introduce Lucozade to the Newcastle medical profession before the war. When he or his men called on doctors they always left a large 26-ounce bottle on the doctor's desk. Hunter's idea was that no one would throw away a large bottle of Lucozade priced at that time at 2s. 3d., and the doctor would either use it himself or give it to a patient in need.

For some time I had been unhappy at the pace of new product introduction. The pattern of *successful* launches seemed to be three years of heavy advertising and substantial losses, with a break-even point at the end of the third year. This used not to be so and I felt that the reason was the sheer volume of advertising now being used and the difficulty of being seen in the forest or heard in the din, unless one spent enormous sums. The launch of Tooth Paste in the U.S.A. brought things to a head. We could not possibly match the expenditures of Colgate and Procter & Gamble and so we had to aim to get the product

tried in the home by other means. Sampling by giving a
tube of Macleans free with a tube of Brylcreem might do it
and, if so, would be relatively cheap because it would help
Brylcreem sales. Then we turned to door-to-door sampling.
We chose to use a large-size tube, partly because of Hunter's
Lucozade theory that no one would fail to try a large size, and
partly because I had always believed that a liking for the
Macleans flavour was a habit which once acquired, would
stick, and I therefore thought we ought to give a large tube. In
the event, we never proved *why* it worked, but it did, and the
curious thing was that demand for Macleans in the store came
very quickly – long before one would expect a large-size tube
to be used up.

It is interesting to compare the Brylcreem and Macleans
launches. It took six years for Brylcreem to reach national
distribution and six years elapsed before it became profitable,
by which time there were $1,770,000 of accumulated losses to
be recovered and this took four years. Macleans obtained
national distribution in two years, became profitable at the end
of three years, and by that time had lost $2,440,000. These
losses were recovered in a little more than a year.

Macleans Tooth Paste reached its peak and 8 per cent of the
market in four years. I am sure that we could not have succeeded without the sampling campaign, but in the U.S.A.
every time you are successful, competitors copy you and we
soon had to face competition from a Colgate copy of Macleans,
launched with similar advertising and sampled at a rate
double ours. This effectively stopped us from ever reaching our
target of 10 per cent of the market and indeed Beechams have
been fighting ever since.

It must be remembered that by the time of the Macleans
launch we had become much more professional, which was just
as well, as we were operating in perhaps the most difficult
market in the U.S.A. Also, at that time, the food stores were
becoming more and more important and many of them were
serviced by 'rack jobbers'. These were organizations that had
contracts with large food chain stores to erect racks in the stores
and stock them with all the best-selling toiletry goods. They

supplied the goods on wholesale terms and the stores took the normal profit. It was argued that the rack jobber knew more about his class of merchandise than the food buyer, and that he would create much more business and therefore profit for the store. The rack jobbers had an arrangement under which they all recorded their sales by means of a standard International Business Machine system. These sales figures were then sent to a central office, added together, divided into areas and the resulting analysis sold to proprietary manufacturers whose goods were purchased for sale on the racks. It was a very fast means of measuring sales results and as the rack jobbers covered a very substantial proportion of the total sales through food stores, the figures were a pretty accurate index of the way total sales were progressing. The charges for the figures made available to manufacturers paid for the cost of the jobbers' accounting system. We bought the analysis and were able to identify the sales of Macleans Tooth Paste and to relate them to the areas where jobbers were stocking Macleans. These figures we drew to the attention of the rack jobbers in new areas and, indeed, rack jobbers in old areas who had refused to go along with us. As a result, we were able to get the vast majority of them to stock and push Macleans by demonstrating that they would achieve a high profit per foot of shelf space used. We did not need a sales force for this – just a few first-class Area Managers, and these we had. I would mention in particular Ken Rosenwald on the West Coast, who set a fine standard in the opening rounds.

And so by 1964–65 we were riding high. The business was making reasonable profits – $2 million on sales of $21 million – all out of Brylcreem. Macleans was rapidly moving out of the red and we were once more turning our attention to shampoos. But we had to withstand the counter-attacks, and they were nasty.

Bristol-Myers Co. had watched the rise of Brylcreem without any noticeable reaction except that they altered and improved the formula of their product, Vitalis. This was a clear liquid hairdressing. Then suddenly they started their 'greasy kid stuff' advertising campaign. This used well-known sportsmen who poured scorn on another player using that 'greasy kid stuff' and they made it obvious that they were referring to Brylcreem. Of course, they then went on to laud Vitalis and to refer to it as greaseless. Vitalis originally contained about 20 per cent of natural castor oil in a strong alcohol base. This was subsequently changed to an oily synthetic material soluble in a less strong alcohol but stickier than the oil used in Brylcreem. Anyhow, we did nothing about this for some time and then Bristol-Myers launched Score, a clear gel, and Chesebrough-Pond's put out Groom & Clean, a product claimed to clean as it groomed. Everyone was now claiming to be greaseless and Brylcreem sales suffered. From a high of $12,453,000 in 1961–62 they fell to $9,480,000 in 1965–66.

Then we came back again. This was, in my opinion, in large part due to the public beginning to discover that the so-called greaseless products were not all they were held out to be. At the same time we had finally got around to an appropriate advertising reply with our 'I came back' copy. This showed young men with the inevitable girl in a situation in which they said that they had tried these gels and liquids but they did not suit their hair and they came back to Brylcreem. We visually demonstrated the difference between hair treated with the 'other' product and Brylcreem and it was true. Sales of Score in particular fell away and Brylcreem sales commenced to climb until in 1968–69 they reached $13,452,000.

Meanwhile, Macleans Tooth Paste sales, which had very quickly jumped to $10 million, climbed to $15 million in 1966–67 and then fell back to $13,399,000 in 1968–69. Sales had been maintained for a time by the launch of an additional spearmint flavour, but we were finding it increasingly difficult to hold our position against all the frantic activity in the market. Prior to the launch of Macleans, I had spoken to several chairmen of major U.S. proprietary companies that had a brand of tooth paste on the market. They all took the same view, that it was impossible to stand up to the 'soapers', i.e. Procter & Gamble and Colgate, and so they were 'milking' their brands (i.e. underspending on advertising and maximizing on profit) thus resigning themselves to the slow demise of their products.

When we launched Macleans we priced it at roughly a 10 per cent premium. At that time such a course was unheard of, but it was necessary if we were to have anything approaching an adequate margin for advertising and profit. Following our success, everyone woke up to the fact that it was possible to live against the soapers if one priced one's product properly.

We ourselves were hardest hit by Colgate with their brand Ultrabrite, a copy of Macleans, but other brands appeared, all launched with massive sampling campaigns and heavy advertising. Bristol-Myers spent many millions on two brands which never achieved a worthwhile share of the market. Then the cosmetic companies got into the act. Alberto Culver launched Mighty White and spent heavily, whilst Hazel Bishop produced Plus White. On top of all this, Lever Brothers (the Unilever subsidiary) put extra advertising behind Pepsodent, a small brand in the U.S.A. with about 3 per cent of the market. This activity stopped us in our tracks and we had to decide whether to meet competition head on and increase our advertising and marketing expenditure substantially, or to wait until the various new contenders had exhausted themselves. We decided to wait, and with hindsight I think we waited too long – and spent too little in the meantime.

By 1967–68 when Beecham Products was merged into Beecham Inc. its sales were $27,785,000 in the U.S.A. and $18,265,000 overseas (Canada, Australia, New Zealand, and South America). Profits were $6,790,000 and we still looked forward to rapid expansion both in the U.S.A. and overseas. This tale will be taken up again in Chapter 16: 'Beecham Inc.'

12 *The Discovery*

Although I had recommended that we set up a Beecham Research Laboratory and had supported Mac to the best of my ability during the early years, I had not been directly responsible for research until, on the appointment of Buckley as Managing Director, the Laboratories were transferred to Macleans. By this time I felt contempt for the name Beecham and the first thing I wanted to do was to change the name to 'Maclean Research Laboratories'. Thank goodness, Mac and Sir Charles Dodds dissuaded me from this step, and so, on my appointment as Managing Director of Beechams, all I had to do was separate Lucozade from Beecham Research Laboratories Ltd. and transfer the company back to Beecham Group Ltd.

I realized that all our futures depended on the Research Laboratories operating successfully and was determined that I was going to be involved in the major decisions. We were working in a number of areas largely on the recommendation of Sir Charles and the other Consultants and, as in all research laboratories, subjects tended to multiply as an observation in one area led to a new project in a related one. I was very anxious to concentrate our efforts but I was no scientist myself and I had to listen to others, principally Mac and Sir Charles.

As has been mentioned, Sir Charles was keen on investigating the amino-acids. These 'bricks' for constructing proteins seemed to him of great importance and he felt that here lay the compounds for the treatment of the ageing body. We became primarily interested in methionine, an amino-acid which had a marked effect on the liver. Sir Charles speculated that whilst it could not cure cirrhosis of the liver, it might protect that organ from further damage. He was himself a 'bon viveur' and I believe contemplated a happy old age guarded by methionine.

SAVAGE CLUB House Dinner
Jan. 6th
1962

In the Chair - Brother Savage

Sir Charles Dodds · M·V·O

Menu
Fillet of Sole
Veronique

Roast Stuffed
Poussin
Château Potatoes
Spinach

Canapé Diane

Coffee

1 CARLTON HOUSE
TERRACE · S·W·1

We were also heavily involved with anti-tubercular drugs about which I was very unhappy. The research staff were clearly spending more and more time in this area, and I did not think that our chances of discovering anything were very great. A vast amount of tubercular work was going on all over the world and our efforts were puny by comparison. Furthermore, there was no one segment into which we could concentrate our efforts. Then Mac came to me and announced that they had discovered a compound with anti-tubercular properties and I was foolish enough to make an announcement to the Board. Subsequently it transpired that the compound was too toxic to consider and I was mortified at making a fool of myself, and research, before the Board.

All this time a small amount of work had been proceeding on penicillin. This flowed from the penicillin pastilles that we had first made for Dr McGregor and had continued to market in a small way. In addition, we were working on formulations which would enable penicillin G to be more readily absorbed when taken orally. This work became uninteresting in 1952 with the discovery of penicillin V which was very well absorbed when taken by mouth.

I had been introduced to, and had become friendly with, Mr William Bristol, one of the Bristol brothers, who between them at that time controlled Bristol-Myers Co. of the U.S.A., the makers of Vitalis, Bufferin, and many other advertised proprietary products. They had commenced the fermentation of penicillin during the war at a new factory in Syracuse in the State of New York. As early as March 1952 I had talked to Bill Bristol about producing penicillin G. He said that he thought he would be ready to help us set up a plant but he advised me to be very careful because the price was continually falling and Bristol-Myers were losing money on their production.

Things came to a head towards the end of 1954. Sir Charles had been talking to us about fermentation chemistry and predicting that more and more compounds would be manufactured by this route. He had named examples of existing production, such as citric acid, and speculated on possibilities for the future, such as the amino-acids and tartaric acid. As a result of these discussions I formed the erroneous view that it was possible to erect a more or less general purpose fermentation plant capable of fermenting penicillin or citric acid or the amino-acids and possibly tartaric acid.

I therefore had a meeting with Mac and Sir Charles and said that I was going to propose that Beechams should, with the help of Bristol-Myers, erect a fermentation plant and that we should commence by producing penicillin G. Sir Charles was very agitated at this, nor was Mac happy, and they went

away to discuss the position. Sir Charles then found an opportunity to talk with Professor Ernst Chain and to his surprise
discovered that Ernst was convinced that there was much
more to discover in the penicillin area. As a result of this, he
and Mac came to see me and made a firm recommendation
that we should seek to engage Professor Chain as a Consultant
and that we should review the whole field of fermentation
chemistry with him before we committed ourselves to a plant.
I was happy to agree to this, not the least because it would
mean that we would have to wind up the T.B. work and a lot
more of little consequence and direct all our energies into
fermentation chemistry.

Ernst Chain was to have a vital influence on Beechams and
it is necessary to pause here and introduce him. He shared the
1945 Nobel Prize for Physiology and Medicine for the penicillin
discovery which revolutionized therapeutic medicine in the
field of bacterial infections. His contribution was two-fold. In
1938 at Oxford he initiated the re-investigation of Fleming's
antibacterial mould which led to the discovery of its remarkable
curative power. Fleming's paper was published in 1929, but it
had not been followed up. Ernst's aim was to study the chemical nature of this antibacterial substance which was apparently
very powerful but was regarded as extremely unstable. Then
he played a leading part in the chemical aspects of the investigation which included the development of sophisticated methods
for its isolation, its purification, and the elucidation of its
chemical structure. The extraction process was patentable and,
in the event, is the only known process of extraction right down
to the present time.

Ernst went to the Secretary of the Medical Research Council and sought permission to take out a patent. He pointed out
that, the work having been carried out by him whilst employed
at Oxford, the patent would belong to the University who
would thus be in a position to control production. The powers-
that-be poured scorn on him for suggesting that a medical
discovery should be patented and stated that such discoveries
were for the benefit of mankind and that it was immoral to
control them by patent. Ernst, always ready to argue, retorted

that having patented the process, Oxford could do what it liked. It could give free licences all over the world if it wished, but at least it would have control. If nothing was done, then others could step in and surround the process with peripheral patents. This would almost certainly mean that Great Britain would lose control; as it did. He continued to argue but achieved nothing by this except to make himself unpopular. What a way to run a country!

In 1948, as a result of his treatment in England, and in particular of the refusal of his masters to provide him with fermentation pilot plant, Ernst took a position with the Instituto Superiore di Sanita in Rome. Here he had erected a complete small-scale fermentation plant and was pursuing his ideas on the development of penicillin.

Sir Charles and Mac began their discussions with Ernst in 1954 and in the course of these I visited him at the Institute in Rome and took an instant liking to him and his delightful wife, who was a fine scientist in her own right, and who also worked at the Institute. Ernst and I are both mavericks and have remained firm friends ever since. Our negotiations with Ernst's lawyers over his consultancy agreement were long and tortuous but these did not hold up our collaboration and we had our first formal meeting attended by some of our consultants, scientists, and commercial men in May 1955. There followed a series of meetings for the purpose of determining the direction our work should take.

In the first instance we examined the possibility of producing tartaric acid by a process involving fermentation. It was produced from argol, the crystalline residue deposited in the vats during fermentation of grape juice to wine and we used large quantities of tartaric acid in Eno's. With increasing affluence there was less incentive for the thousands of small growers in Italy and Spain to take their relatively small quantities of argol into market. The quantities available were falling and the price therefore increasing. On top of all this we were faced with the fact that if we were able to expand the sales of Eno's in the U.S.A. even to half the *per capita* sales in Canada, we would need to double our purchases of tartaric acid and we already took about one-third of the total world supply! For a time it looked as though this would be the means of our entering the area of fermentation chemistry but gradually it became clear that to evolve a process would mean making a major effort and that the chances of success – that is, of finding a process cheap enough – were slim. We held a series of most important meetings at Pall Mall on 19 and 20 September 1955 and I set out here the full minutes of the two afternoon meetings. The meeting on the morning of the 19th was a scientific one at which we decided that work on tartaric acid had to be deferred and that we should concentrate on penicillin.

Confidential

Minutes of Two Meetings held at 68 Pall Mall
at 2.30 p.m. on Monday, 19th September, 1955
and 2.30 p.m. on Tuesday, 20th September, 1955

PRESENT: Mr. H. G. Lazell – in the Chair.
Sir Charles Dodds
Sir Ian Heilbron (Tuesday meeting).
Dr. E. B. Chain.
Mr. W. McGeorge.
Mr. N. F. Fabricius (part-time).
Mr. C. D. W. Stafford.
Dr. J. Farquharson.
Mr. R. Towell.

Mr. Lazell summarised the position reached after the morning meeting. For some time discussions had taken place on entry into the microbiological field as it appeared of such importance that it could no longer be ignored. Originally, a research unit had been considered which would investigate materials already in use by the Group and from that point discussions had centred on tartaric acid. It now appeared that there were difficulties with tartaric acid in that the first method considered appeared to be so expensive that it was not worth further consideration, a second method which was proposed could only be considered as long-term. If this were pursued too long then work would neither be done on microbiological materials for sale nor on antibiotics. If those present really believed in microbiological production it was necessary to go straight in, otherwise the growth of the Group's ethical business would always be limited. The position appeared to be one in which the Group must face up to entering the antibiotic field. In the U.K. the big producers were Glaxo and Distillers, both with methods based on U.S. companies, neither of which was first in the field. There was no doubt that Pfizer were first and Bristol-Myers second. He was in a position to enter into discussions with Bristol-Myers who were not advising other companies in the U.K. They might even give a concession on tetracycline. The evidence was that the U.K. bulk production was of an annual value of the order of £10 million. The type of plant envisaged would have a production some one-eighth of the total. The big question was cost of production, and the key to this was yield. The basic decision was whether to enter the field of antibiotics with the object of gaining a proportionate share of the market.

Mr Stafford agreed that it would be a most attractive proposition to enter the antibiotic field.

Mr. Lazell pointed out that it would be necessary to start with penicillin but it must be at a competitive price. If C. L. Bencard were in a position to produce one-eighth of the total U.K. production at a comparative bulk price to Glaxo then it should be possible to market it. Did Mr. Stafford agree that the project was within the capacity of C. L. Bencard? The decisions to be taken were:—

(1) To plan production based primarily on Antibiotics.
(2) To look for a site for C. L. Bencard where the whole organisation would be in one area.
(3) To adjust research effort such that an adequate effort would be devoted to microbiological research.

Mr. Stafford was of the opinion that C. L. Bencard must get into the field. If the project were based on penicillin, he would have to know the cost differential.

141

Mr. Lazell was of the opinion that Glaxo was probably not more efficient than Merck and Dr. Chain had confirmed that his production figures were 30 per cent better than Merck's. Dr. Chain was of the opinion that it would be possible to keep ahead by combination of new techniques and a genetic approach.

Mr. Lazell felt that he was not now afraid of the cost of the plant at £500,000. This would represent a minimum expenditure and there would be no need to expand until adequate profits were achieved. The plant would be a versatile one and it might be possible to do a deal with Bristol-Myers.

Dr. Chain reported that he had information indicating that the three large Italian producers, Squibb, Leo and Lepetit were all expanding production. All used large fermentors. He thought he could obtain information regarding their production. Mr. Lazell felt that the information really required was the export prices from U.S., Italy, France and that an attempt should be made to obtain these.

At this point it was agreed to go forward with the project subject to Mr. Stafford's detailed examination and subsequent agreement. The following actions were proposed:—

Mr. Lazell.   To have preliminary discussions with Bristol-Myers during his forthcoming visit to the U.S. and to obtain, if possible, information on current yields.

Mr. Stafford: (1) To examine the project in more detail.
(2) To make preliminary enquiries as to a site for a factory, due attention being given to effluent disposal and to Central and Local Government support.
(3) To initiate a project designed to develop new oral products based on purchased material.

Dr. Chain: (1) To prepare a memorandum for Mr. Lazell detailing the types of question which might be used in discussions with Bristol-Myers.

(2) To supply information to Mr. Stafford:
    (a) Detailed lists and current prices in Italy of all raw materials used in the manufacture of penicillin.
    (b) Details of recovery rates for solvents expressed as a percentage of the totals used.
    (c) Details of yields based on the usage of the materials in (a).

(3) To prepare a memorandum on current oral preparations, on chemically modified penicillins and to arrange to attend a discussion on the purely chemical problems at Brockham Park on or about 16th–17th November.

Mr. McGeorge: To arrange for Mr. Husband to:—

(1) Reinvestigate the building costs in the light of Dr. Chain's information that of the four main parts of the process (a) the fermentation building, (b) the extraction and recrystallisation building, (c) the boiler and compressor house and (d) workshops and laboratories, (a) and (c) may be of steel and corrugated asbestos with chequer plate mezzanine floors, whilst (b) and (d) should be of steel and concrete or brick with flame-proof equipment in (b).

(2) Obtain prices for the importation of plant from Italy.

(3) Obtain costs of modern tunnel-type aseptic filling equipment with details of performance and operatives required (with Mr. Stafford).

Dr. Farquharson: (1) To recruit three Microbiologists (Biochemists) to commence work in Rome on 1st January, 1956.

143

(2) To prepare a master plan of the extension of the pilot plant buildings to provide laboratory and pilot plant accommodation for microbiological research.

(3) To produce a plan designed to adjust the research at Brockham Park such that an adequate effort would be devoted to microbiological work.

Following these decisions, when I next visited the U.S.A. I had discussions with Mr Fred Schwartz, then the President of Bristol Laboratories, the Pharmaceutical Division of Bristol-Myers Co. He again expressed their readiness to put us into production of penicillin G but warned me that they themselves were not making any profit out of it. He agreed with my basic view that we should endeavour to enter the field of fermentation chemistry, but could not suggest how, other than to produce penicillin G.

Doug Stafford completed his investigations. He agreed with me that Glaxo must be making profits and speculated that Pfizer and Merck were probably the most efficient producers. Glaxo had a licence from Merck and paid them a royalty.

I had agreed with Mac and Sir Charles that we would give research two years to produce something before we put up a penicillin G fermentation plant. I have no doubt that this was the most sensible decision and in the event it did not make much difference. We had no facilities when our discovery enabled us to produce the molecular core of penicillin and for two years had to buy all our supplies from Bristol-Myers. However, whilst I had agreed to give research two years before we put up a plant, we did commence our search for a site that would be suitable for a fermentation factory. I quote from a report I made to the Board on 21 December 1955:

Micro-Biological Research

The memorandum from Mr McGeorge was received. Mr Lazell pointed out that these proposals involved additional

144

expenditure on research amounting to approximately £15,000 in the first year and that they would involve capital expenditure of the order of £65,000. If this research resulted in a valuable and patentable invention, the Group would then be faced by the need for capital expenditure of some £500,000 on plant and buildings in order to exploit it to the full. It would also be necessary to move the business of C. L. Bencard Ltd. to a site where micro-biological production could be carried out, and this move should be undertaken in the near future. He explained that in addition to the possibility of an entirely new product being produced microbiologically, there was also the valuable possibility that certain materials of which the Group were large users (e.g. tartaric acid) could be produced micro-biologically instead of chemically as at present. Supplies of tartaric acid were currently controlled by a ring and the Group were the largest users in the United Kingdom.

If anyone had suggested that we should have to spend on Capital Account not £500,000 but £5 million (and much more later on) I wonder what would have been said.

We knew that Pfizer, the U.S. company, were erecting a fermentation factory at Sandwich on the south coast of England and we fixed on Worthing as an appropriate place for our plant. The local authority was quite co-operative but we had a lot of trouble with the Board of Trade who wanted us to go north. This would have meant an unacceptable separation from Brockham Park and so we began the tedious negotiations that, in the event, cleared the way for us to commence construction soon after our momentous discovery of the penicillin core and almost immediately we had signed our agreement with Bristol-Myers.

Having decided not to make our first effort in the area of tartaric acid production, we turned to Ernst's ideas on penicillin and here we soon reached agreement on what should be done. He recommended that we arranged for some key staff to be seconded to his laboratories at the Istituto di Sanita in Rome for indoctrination into his methods and ideas. Four of our scientists were sent there including two whose names were subsequently associated with our discovery: Dr George Rolinson, a microbiologist who had just joined us from Boots where he had been employed on penicillin, and Ralph Batchelor, a biochemist who came to us from Cambridge University via the Water Pollution Research Laboratories in Surrey.

By this time our research organization had a very strong Chemistry Department including Peter Doyle and John Nayler, whose names, together with those mentioned above, appeared on our basic patent. We also had a strong Pharmacology Department led by David Brown with the animal houses required for the assessment and testing of potential new compounds, and smaller Departments of Bacteriology, Biochemistry, and Physical Chemistry necessary for the efficient progress of such research. There was no Department of Chemical Microbiology, which would be needed for any work on penicillin, and we were therefore only in a position to work on the chemical manipulation of the penicillin molecule. Chain's idea was that we should begin by making para-aminobenzyl penicillin. This was a very stable entity and he believed that it would lend itself to chemical manipulation which would, hopefully, give us new compounds of therapeutic value.

The work proceeded at Rome and we began to erect at Brockham Park a duplicate of Ernst Chain's small-scale fermentation plant. Rome had produced a kilogram of para-aminobenzyl penicillin, and the pilot fermentation plant at Brockham was now being brought into full operation to provide further quantities for the research team.

In the course of 1957, on an increasing number of occasions, it was observed that chemical and biological assays for the penicillin content of experimental broths gave different results. This was not an entirely new observation, but it had previously been ascribed to experimental error. Now, however, a pattern was noted. The discrepancy was greatest when no precursor was added to the medium in which the penicillium mould was growing and declined as quantities of precursors were increased.

Discussions among our four scientists produced two alternative hypotheses. Either there was a penicillin in the broth which had little or no effect on bacteria, or there was present the molecular core of penicillin, 6-amino-penicillanic acid (6-APA), lacking the characteristic side chain of ordinary penicillins. Other research workers had postulated that such a core was a step in the growth of all penicillins, but the substance had never been isolated. Indeed, it was thought if the hypothesis was right that 6-APA would be too unstable to extract.

Assuming that 6-APA was present, the chemists argued, it would be possible by a simple process to convert it to penicillin G. This experiment was carried out at the end of May 1957 and penicillin G was, in fact, found to have been produced. It was a momentous result. The strong presumption, amounting almost to a certainty that 6-APA was present, meant that now the whole research programme had to take a new turn. Complete proof was established by chromatographic techniques during the succeeding month, and from then on all possible effort was devoted to devising ways of extracting 6-APA in a pure form. This was not achieved until January 1958, but then we were faced with the problem of the minute quantity of 6-APA present in the early broths. At that time the total fermenter capacity at Brockham was 90 gallons and it produced only seven-tenths of an ounce of pure 6-APA in one run. Once stable 6-APA was in the hands of the chemists they could start adding an almost infinite number of side chains at will. There was practically no limit to the number and there was a good chance, though no certainty, that among the many new compounds which could be made, there would be a number which would greatly extend the range of penicillin therapy.

For a long time there was much doubt about how to proceed. On 17 March 1958 Sir Ian Heilbron (one of our Consultants) was reported as doubting that 6-APA could be produced in quantity by a microbiological route and suggesting that a potential synthetic route be examined. At the same meeting other research projects were discussed and on reading these old minutes I am reminded of my demands to Mac that we concentrate *all* our efforts on the new penicillins. He had to explain to me that some of our scientists were just not qualified for the penicillin work and that anyway we had to proceed by orderly stages. There were admittedly many imponderables to be studied and what looks obvious now was not so in those days. But it remains true that we had nowhere near enough skilled manpower or facilities to work at the speed the circumstances demanded.

The most economic process for production of 6-APA was the subject of discussion and argument for a long time. On the one hand it could be produced by direct fermentation. On the other it could be obtained by splitting off the side chain of penicillin V by chemical means. However, whatever process we used we should want a factory capable of fermenting 6-APA or penicillin and carrying out the various chemical processes needed. We had our site at Worthing and all we needed was the necessary know-how for constructing the plant and the final 'permits' and consents from Government.

We had enlarged our small-scale plant at Brockham and by June 1958 we had a recovery rate for 6-APA of 45 per cent; there was 15 grams of solid 6-APA available and we commenced the preparation of new penicillins at a rate of about twelve per month. Provisional and/or final patent applications had been made for 6-APA itself, for certain processes, and for the compounds we had made and tested. It was now considered by the scientists that the time had come for publication and no doubt everyone was itching to do this. Scientists are as much concerned with fame as with money and they were all fearful that someone else would get in first. The first I knew of this was when Mac came to me in December and revealed that a paper was due to be published in *Nature* in January or February 1959. I was furious and demanded that it be withdrawn pending discussions that I proposed to have with Fred Schwartz of Bristol-Myers, but was told that it was impossible to withdraw as it was in the hands of the Editor. Anyway one of the Belgian patents was due to be published in January.

Everyone admitted that we were too inexperienced and too small to go it alone in the U.S.A. and I had been waiting until our patent position was more secure before approaching Bristol-Myers for discussions. Looking back it is clear that I waited too long. I had chosen Bristol-Myers because I had a high opinion of the Bristol brothers and considered that they were gentlemen who could be relied on to see that we tyros were dealt with fairly and honourably. In addition, they had already expressed a readiness to help us erect a fermentation plant, to teach us how to use it, and to put us into production. This would be of inestimable value to us. I therefore asked Mac to write at once to Fred Schwartz setting out our discovery and enclosing copies of the papers so that we could have a full discussion when I got to the U.S.A. in January. Mac wrote on 30 December and early in January came into my office very crestfallen with a letter from Fred Schwartz saying that Bristol-Myers were 'de-emphasizing' their penicillin work and that whilst he would pass Mac's letter on to his scientists he did not think that they would be interested! All the doubts and fears of the tuberculosis period welled up in my mind but, fortunately, we did not have long to bite our nails, for that afternoon a cable arrived from Schwartz expressing great interest and asking how soon we could visit him. His scientists at Syracuse had immediately seen the importance of our discovery and they were awaiting our trip with impatience.

We arrived in New York soon afterwards and almost immediately attended meetings at Bristol-Myers' head office. I was accompanied by Mac and Stuart Updike, our U.S. lawyer, and we were faced by Fred Schwartz, who was now Pesident of the parent company, Bristol-Myers Co., Phil Bowman, the President of Bristol Laboratories, and a team from the Bristol-Myers legal department. I was disconcerted by the course of these negotiations and gradually realized that Fred, whilst professing eternal friendship, was going to strike the hardest bargain he could.

I cannot remember in detail all our negotiations with Bristol and in any event it would be tedious to recount them. Our lawyers continued to argue about the detailed drafting after I returned to England, during which time we were visited by most of the big American drug houses. We might well have dropped Bristol if one of the others had been ready to teach us the fermentation business and put us into production, but none of them would and so we finally signed. This roughly gave Bristol an exclusive licence under our patents in the U.S. subject to our right, alone or in partnership, to enter the market. They also had a licence under our patents to sell in the rest of the world outside the British Commonwealth. In return for this they agreed to pay us a royalty of 5 per cent, to set their laboratories to work in producing compounds all of which were to be our property, and to train our personnel and control the erection of an antibiotic factory at Worthing. We were to have long and frustrating arguments with Bristol over the terms of this agreement but I have nothing but praise for the way in which they carried out their obligations in regard to the factory. Our men were treated magnificently in the U.S.A. and Bristol sent a fine team to operate at Worthing who handed the factory over to us in first-class order. Thus in 1961 we at last had our fermentation factory.

I have here touched only briefly on the discovery and development of penicillin itself. Anyone wishing to pursue it in detail should read the paper by Sir Ernst Chain: 'Thirty years of penicillin therapy,' *Proc. Roy. Soc. Lond.*, B.179, 293–319 (1971).

13 *After Ten Years*

Looking back it can be said that January 1962 marked a time in the affairs of Beecham Group when the tide of success, previously running strongly along the advertised proprietary products channel, altered course and thereafter ran with increasing strength along the pharmaceutical channel. On that date, the Group was divided into three Divisions, all with worldwide control of its product categories. The organization chart published in the Annual Report for 1961–62 set out the new arrangement and is shown overleaf. This did not last long as we soon separated the Western Hemisphere again. It will be noticed that we still retained the individual company structure and in consequence we still needed our accounting section at Headquarters, specializing in 'consolidation' of the accounts for year-end and financial reporting purposes. It was not until 1964 that we moved to true divisionalization when we merged all the individual home companies into Beecham Group Ltd. and either wound them up or kept them as 'name' companies shorn of all assets and liabilities.

N. F. Fabricius had died in October 1960 and in 1963 John Rintoul had a heart attack and died a young man. Thus the senior management had been decimated. The loss of John was a bitter blow to me personally and to all his friends. It left a great hole in our administration just when we needed more strength. The new organization was supposed to bring about my withdrawal from 'front line' operations in our proprietary business and in particular my heavy participation in the marketing and advertising policies of the main products, Lucozade, Brylcreem (mainly overseas), Macleans Tooth Paste, and Eno's. The Group had become much larger and the appearance of a Pharmaceutical Division which we expected to grow very rapidly made for more complexity and called for more financial control at the top. Clearly, I ought to spend more of my time at Headquarters and on pharmaceutical affairs, particularly in the U.S.A. This made it impossible to do a proper marketing job.

	BEECHAM GROUP LIMITED	
BEECHAM FOOD AND DRINK DIVISION LTD.	BEECHAM TOILETRY DIVISION LTD.	BEECHAM PHARMACEUTICAL DIVISION LTD.
Beecham Foods Ltd.	County Laboratories Ltd.	Beecham Research Laboratories Ltd.
Thomas & Evans Ltd.	Beecham Overseas Ltd.	Beecham Proprietary Medicines Ltd.
James Pascall Ltd.	*Overseas Companies* Beecham (Argentina) S.A.C.I.	Beecham
Coca-Cola Northern Bottlers Ltd.	Beecham (Australia) Pty. Ltd. Beecham-Denmark A/S Beecham de Mexico S.A.	Pharmaceutical Exports Ltd.
Beecham Food Export Ltd.	Beecham (Far East) Ltd. Beecham (France) Ltd. Beecham (India) Private Ltd.	Overseas concessionaires and licensees
Overseas Companies James Pascall (Ireland) Ltd. James Pascall (S.A.) (Pty) Ltd.	Beecham (Malaya) Ltd. Beecham (Nederland) N.V. Beecham (Pakistan) Ltd. Beecham Products Inc. (U.S.A.) Beecham Products Ltd. (Canada) Beecham S.A. (Belgium)	
Overseas concessionaires	Beecham (Sales) Ltd. (Ireland) Beecham South Africa (Pty.) Ltd. Eno-Scott & Bowne (Cuba) Ltd. Eno-Scott & Bowne (Venezuela) Ltd. Laboratories Beecham S.A. (Brazil)	
	Overseas concessionaires	

Organization Chart for 1962

To my mind, marketing is an art that calls for total immersion in the subject. I once heard an apocryphal story of an executive in a U.S. advertising agency who attended a meeting on a cigarette account one day and pulled out a pack of a competing brand. The Account Director saw the pack and said, 'Al, do you want to eat?' Al looked confused and apologized, explaining that he had left home hurriedly and by mistake had picked up his wife's cigarettes. The Account Director's only reply was, 'Does your wife want to eat?' I personally believe that where possible one should be a user of the product. At home we certainly used Lucozade, Eno's, Macleans Tooth Paste, and a number of our other products; I was also a 'Brylcreem boy'.

To function properly in marketing in our fields one has to attend Nielsen briefings, where they go thoroughly into what is happening in the market place, and trace the results of one's own and one's competitors actions. Then it is helpful to analyse related markets in the same way. In addition, one must be concerned with consumer research, take part in the discussions on what enquiries should be pursued and the replies received. Then it is most important to sit in at marketing meetings at the company's offices and to listen to the line executives. Finally, one must participate in all major review meetings with the advertising agents. This takes a lot of time and clearly I was no longer able to function properly in this area.

Bay Houchen became Chairman of Beecham Food and Drink Division Ltd. and he had a strong administrative and technical team under him, led by Jack Smartt who was Managing Director of Beecham Foods Ltd. and Jim Sullivan, who as Technical Director of the management company over-saw the whole production and distributive field. Bay's marketing men were not so strong.

Beecham Pharmaceutical Division Ltd. represented the concentration of all our pharmaceutical interests, including the advertised medicines, under one management which was headed by Doug Stafford. He had Bob Wilkins as Managing Director of Beecham Research Laboratories Ltd. and Frank Lomax as Managing Director of Beecham Pharmaceutical Exports Ltd. These two, and the men operating under them, were first class. As will be explained later, they were mostly hand-picked by Doug to make up the team to develop our new penicillins. Then we had Joe Davies leading Beecham Proprietary Medicines Ltd. and Bill Ambrose as Marketing Director. Bill knew the 'medicine' business inside out. This business eventually finished up with the rest of our advertised proprietary products where it did much better.

Finally, we set up Beecham Toiletry Division Ltd. with new

and heavier responsibilities. I had appointed Tony, the son of N. F. Fabricius, Chairman of this Division and made him responsible for toiletries worldwide. For this purpose I had resigned as Chairman of Beecham Products Inc. and appointed Tony in my place. Then I had transferred Maurice Bale to England making him Vice-Chairman of the Division and Marketing Director, and he was accompanied by Ed Rose from Canada, who became Operations Director, Western Hemisphere and Australasia. The two existing Marketing Vice-Presidents in the U.S.A. and Canada were appointed Presidents and new men brought in. Thus, for the first time since I had become the Chief Executive, the Western Hemisphere ceased to be my personal responsibility and became part of the Toiletry Division. It was because overall responsibility had been transferred to Tony, and also so as to bolster toiletry marketing throughout the world, particularly in the U.K., that I brought Maurice Bale and Ed Rose to England. Tony was a young man of ability but I was afraid that I was forcing him. I felt that if I supported him with sufficient ability, particularly on the marketing side, he would make good.

The new worldwide Toiletries Division never worked properly. Tony was overwhelmed by the weight of his problems which unfortunately were many and heavy. The newly promoted men in the U.S.A. and Canada were not showing the capacity to rule and both markets were in trouble. In the U.S.A. there was the record deal to clear up and the launch of Tooth Paste looming. In Canada, Tooth Paste was on the market and Silvikrin Shampoo had been established but was unprofitable. Both Maurice Bale and Ed Rose were undertaking functional responsibility for the first time and seemed like fish out of water. As was my usual habit, I had only painted the canvas depicting my idea of their organization with a very broad brush, but now there was no John Rintoul to add the detail, grease the wheels, and make everything work.

I was always quoting what I alleged was Napoleon's dictum – 'I will give my enemy anything but time' – and once I was convinced that something had to be done I moved quickly. Tony Fabricius resigned on 31 March 1963 and I assumed temporary charge of the Toiletry Division (which subsequently went to Bob Murphy who had been the Administrative Director). Then I again broke off the Western Hemisphere, resumed the Chairmanship of Beecham Products Inc., and sent Maurice Bale back to assume the Presidency once more. I also sent Ed Rose back to resume charge of the Canadian company. This move was, I believe, inevitable in all the circumstances. It reduced the size of each operation and therefore made every job easier. However, it did not solve my problems and meant that never again could I be thorough enough in the marketing area. Of course, it also established beyond doubt that the demands of the Pharmaceutical Division on our best executive blood had resulted in damage to our proprietary business. This continued to be so until we were able to move Ronnie Halstead back to the U.K. and put him in charge first of Beecham Food and Drink Division and, later, of Beecham Products Division, which controlled both Food and Drink and Toiletries everywhere but in the Western Hemisphere. By this time he was greatly aided first by the acquisition of Don McLure, who turned out to be a top-class marketing man, and by the steady growth in stature of Jim Sullivan, the finest organizer the Group has ever had.

The accounts for the year to March 1962 showed the following comparison with those to March 1952:

		1952 (£m.)	1962 (£m.)
Sales	U.K.	10·06	38·98
	Overseas	8·43	19·65
		18·49	58·63
Profits	U.K.	1·36	5·60
	Overseas	1·25	2·31
		2·61	7·91

The small rise in overseas profits in relation to increased sales was, of course, due to the development expenditure in the U.S.A. and, in particular, to losses on the record deals I spoke about in Chapter 11.

It is interesting to compare the profits relating to those brands which had made the largest contribution to our progress and I set them out hereunder:

		1952 (£)	1962 (£)
Brylcreem	Sales	2,643,918	10,584,676
	Profits	415,529	1,970,514
Lucozade	Sales	1,499,788	4,206,852
	Profits	362,077	1,031,164
Eno's 'Fruit Salt'	Sales	2,366,923	3,418,631
	Profits	415,529	504,504
Macleans Tooth Paste	Sales	1,756,819	3,922,402
	Profits*	211,826	348,786
Beecham's Powders	Sales	317,375	1,454,527
	Profits	93,655	436,323
Phensic	Sales	328,764	1,157,230
	Profits	61,535	299,547
Antibiotics	Sales	Nil	3,100,225
	Profits and Royalties		901,655

* Tooth Paste profits were affected by U.S. development expenditure and did not reach £1 million until some time later.

We had made a number of important acquisitions. There was Ribena and Quosh with the business of H. W. Carter & Co. Ltd. in 1955; Vosene Medicated Shampoo with the business of Vosemar Ltd. (1955); Corona soft drinks with the business of Thomas & Evans Ltd. (1958); PLJ with the The Pure Lemon Juice Co. Ltd. (1958); Pascalls confectionery with James Pascall Ltd. (1959); and Du Lundi with a range of deodorants, including Body Mist (1959).

I have already referred to the fact that we had to bid against Reckitt & Colman for Carters, and against Schweppes for Thomas & Evans. All the other acquisitions were agreed with the principal shareholders. We never considered the acquisition of a business unless we could see an opportunity for rationalization and consequent higher efficiency, both in the new business and in ours. I do not believe that there is any justification for acquiring a business and then letting it run on as before. I know that conglomerates argue that by acquiring businesses and providing them with better management they are performing a useful economic service. Perhaps where management has been deplorable this can be done, but I do not subscribe to the theory that 'management' is a science in itself and can be applied to any business with success. My life at the top of Beechams has certainly convinced me that experience counts for a lot. I have known men who could manage a soap business very effectively but who would make an awful mess of a proprietary medicine or a toiletry business. Again, successful management of a pharmaceutical company or division calls for a very different animal. It can, I suppose, be argued that top management in a conglomerate seeks out the men with the appropriate experience and merely applies rational financial control but, again, the more diverse the operations, the more difficult everything becomes, even financial control. Anyway, if they have the power, financial men cannot resist the temptation to interfere with operations. Most of them have an inbred contempt for the marketing men. To my mind, therefore, acquisitions should facilitate concentration of management into compatible divisions. There is a continuing tendency for every business to become more and more complex and top management must counter this by constantly endeavouring to simplify and by being prepared to shed those parts of the business that have become insignificant or disparate.

In our case, Ribena and PLJ took their place alongside Lucozade in Beecham Foods as 'health drinks' and were marketed by the same team. They were near relations to proprietary medicines. Quosh, which was a brand applied to a range of squashes, principally an orange squash, was heavily promoted by Beecham Foods in a sustained effort to win a substantial share of this important market. We were in direct competition with Schweppes, Lyons, Reckitt & Colman, and Unilever and we had a hard time for some years before we finally reached a profitable position. By that time we had developed, and were selling in quantity, canned drinks to grocers under the Hunts and Idris labels and also canned Coca-Cola.

Vosene became our dandruff shampoo and did very well in England. I always regarded it as our best shampoo but I could not persuade the U.S. executive to this view and there, and in other overseas markets where it was tried, it failed. In my view these efforts were either half-hearted or so many differences were made in the formula, pack, and advertising, that we were selling a different product.

Commercial television was introduced in 1955 and after the initial furore the various programme companies started to lose money at an alarming rate. The trouble was that the rates then being charged were not justified because there were too few sets on the market capable of receiving the commercial stations and therefore too few people saw the advertising. Many advertising agencies were advising their clients not to venture their money on television until the number of viewers increased. Beechams only spent experimental sums and we were, of course, courted by the television companies.

I kept a careful eye on the viewership figures. I was waiting until it was possible to buy at a reasonable price segments of time which would result in the advertisements for every one of our brands being seen by a minimum of 20 per cent of total television homes four times a month. This was the standard we adopted in the U.S.A. and I knew that it worked. Towards the end of 1956 it became possible and I asked Charles Truefitt of Associated Rediffusion (one of the London stations) to see me.

When he came I offered him a bulk contract from Beechams for, I believe, £250,000 covering a six-months' period at rates nearly half the standard rates prevailing. This was accepted and in due course the other companies approached us and we made similar contracts with them. In a remarkably short time other businesses followed us and almost overnight the television companies moved from making heavy losses to making large profits. I always claimed that they had me to thank for this dramatic turn around but of course it would have happened anyway; nevertheless, Beechams got there first. But for us I do not think that it would have been quite so dramatic.

Our sudden surge into television did all our brands a lot of good, especially where our competitors stayed out. This was particularly true of Murraymints. Mortons owned a small confectionery business called R. S. Murray & Co. Ltd. This company disposed of a small sales force concentrated in the south of England. It marketed a small range of confectionery which included Murraymints, a wrapped boiled sweet. Sales of Murraymints were quite buoyant and we determined to advertise them on television. Bensons were employed as agents and they produced the famous series of television commercials, showing marching bands playing and singing the jingle:

> *Murraymints, Murraymints,*
> *The Too-Good-To-Hurry Mints,*
> *Why make haste*
> *When you can taste*
> *The hint of Mint in Murraymints.*

Sales of Murraymints soared and the brand became quite well known. This revived our interest in confectionery. It was an enormous market dominated by Cadbury Fry but with Rowntrees, Mars, and Mackintoshes also holding substantial shares. It was obvious that we were not going to make any money unless we had a much larger business but then in 1959 I was introduced to the Pascall family, who were prepared to sell James Pascall Ltd. In spite of the fact that profits were negligible we decided to buy and attempt to build a substantial confectionery business. Murrays was merged with Pascalls, and Bay Houchen was made Chairman of the Company, so as to associate it with Beecham Foods. We set up confectionery development laboratories, transferred some good marketing men, authorized development expenditure and an increased sales force and substantial advertising, but all to little effect.

Other confectionery houses were now spending money on TV. It was soon apparent that Pascalls was not nearly big enough to give us the production or selling efficiency that was required. Moreover, boiled sweets were the least buoyant end of the confectionery market and it became clear that our bright young marketeers did not know enough about confectionery and could not stand up to the old hands in the market.

We gave some thought to making a more serious effort and rounding off our company by acquiring a chocolate and a toffee business. However, I was not successful in persuading

Mackintoshes to join us and so we decided to get out. This was in July 1964 and we now knew that we had a 'horse by the tail' in our pharmaceutical business. It was probably wise for us to rely on internal growth in our proprietary business and to leave acquisitions until the pharmaceutical explosion had settled a bit. So Bay Houchen approached Cadbury Fry, and in due course settled the terms of a sale of our whole confectionery business to them. They were delightful people to deal with, quickly agreed to terms that looked after staff, particularly old employees, and I am glad to say everything went through smoothly and we never had a cross word.

The business of Du Lundi came to us from South Africa. In 1959 the Chief Executive of the Philip Hill South African branch came to see me to enquire whether we were interested in acquiring Du Lundi. It had a big business there, selling a range of liquid deodorants and cheap perfumes. Our South African management was very keen and we agreed to purchase. We were anxious to enter the deodorant market and we put several Du Lundi products out in the U.K. Body Mist was an instant success and went on to win nearly 30 per cent of the total market. I tried to put it out in the U.S.A. but our people there were never enthusiastic. However, later on we launched it in Brazil and Venezuela and again did sensationally well. We were very late getting into the deodorant market and Body Mist helped us catch up.

There were other acquisitions made after 1962 but during my remaining term of office none as important as those made before that date. Since I have retired, of course, there has been the Horlicks business in the U.K. and Fischer & Fischer in Germany, both very important. Then Beechams finally purchased Massengill in the U.S.A. which I had failed to get in 1965.

During the ten years we had greatly increased our stature in the home market. Lucozade and Ribena were widely known and respected. Then there were Brylcreem, Macleans Tooth Paste, Beecham's Powders, and the shampoos, all either dominating or taking a respectable share of their market. On top of this the development of Coca-Cola and the acquisition of Corona and Quosh had established us as a force in the soft drink market. Our success in the U.S.A. had been of particular benefit to our image and with this and our success in other overseas markets we could properly claim to be one of the few truly international British companies.

Finally, there was the announcement of our momentous antibiotic discovery made in 1959, which the financial pundits now saw presented us with unique opportunities.

The business itself had greatly changed. No one was able to dig a comfortable hole and relax. We had frequent 'reorganizations' and people were switched around. I was often warned that under this treatment morale would crack, but I was convinced that morale always held up if you were successful. The only time spirits sagged in Beechams was during the years when we were in trouble. This occurred in Beecham Foods during their early troubles in 1955–56 and again in 1962–63 when they were badly hit by the imposition of purchase tax on soft drinks. Then morale slumped in Beecham Inc. in 1961–62 when the record deals went wrong, but recovered to an all-time high with the success of Tooth Paste.

Management was our big problem. My early years as a junior accountant in Allen & Hanburys had resulted in some strongly held views on this subject. I believed that to be kind and soft with managers who had proved to be inadequate merely resulted in hardship for the rank and file. In those days they were the people who paid the price if business fell off and if profits were inadequate. If therefore one paid proper regard to the interests of the mass of the workers, one found that they were the same as the shareholders and one *had* to be ruthless with the inadequate manager.

I always tried to temper this with generous terminal payments and our pension scheme was structured to give, to those who left, paid-up pensions at age 65 in respect of all years of service with the company. We had some able managers from the businesses acquired, some of whom I have mentioned or shall mention, but our rapid expansion created vacuums at the top and inevitably some good men were sucked into them and overtaxed. I could not leave them where they were and I never believed it wise to demote people. As a result they had to go and were lost to the business. We brought in a number of executives with varying degrees of success. I do not think it is possible to dogmatize in this area, but we certainly were most successful when we recruited senior management from outside only into second-line positions where it was possible for them to acquire a feel of the business and where top management was able to make a careful appraisal of their abilities.

I became convinced that it would only be possible to meet the needs of the business if we developed our own management team and this was one of the Personnel Department's most important functions. It was made clear to all managers that it was one of their responsibilities to make sure that they had an adequate successor. Whoever it was had to be named and Personnel had to agree. We also instituted annual appraisal reports on all executive staff which had to be completed by immediate superiors and approved by their superiors and by Personnel.

Then we formulated our management development policy. The Personnel Departments of Divisions were responsible for all appointments up to a certain level. They had a direct line of responsibility to the Chairman of the Division and a functional line of responsibility to the Group Personnel Director. Group policy had to be observed and in certain categories of staff all appointments had to be made through Headquarters. This applied to all senior executives and to university graduates other than scientists for research. Basically, our policy was to recruit young men from the universities, from public schools, and also from grammar schools. I was a great believer in mixing people and letting them compete. This included encouraging promotion from the lower ranks. Young men, particularly laboratory assistants, were encouraged to take evening classes and gain qualifications. Travellers were given opportunities for promotion and we did everything we could to encourage free competition and promotion on merit.

Naturally, whilst this policy was pursued by Personnel, individual prejudice often frustrated it. The Chartered Accountants in the business did their best to see that we engaged only

Chartered Accountants. On one or two occasions the Association of Certified and Corporate Accountants, of which I was a member, drew my attention to Beecham advertisements for 'Chartered' Accountants, and although on every occasion I made an issue of it both with the offending office (usually Headquarters) and with Personnel, I was under no illusion that prejudice would not continue to raise its ugly head. It is, however, interesting to note that Bill Petley, the finest Financial Director I have ever worked with, came up the hard way and qualified as a Certified Accountant.

Recruitment of scientists was a specialized operation and needed the attention of our top scientists, who maintained close contact with the universities. John Farquharson, our Director of Research from October 1952 to March 1962 and, prior to that, Mac's assistant, made a fine contribution and was largely responsible for the high quality of scientists in our employ at the time of the penicillin discovery. It was not easy to persuade good scientists to join Beechams in the early days and it was a great tribute to John Farquharson and to our Consultants, particularly Sir Ian Heilbron, that we were able to acquire such high-class minds as Peter Doyle, John Nayler, George Rolinson, and Ralph Batchelor. The discovery made it much easier to employ good scientists and from then on it was a question of making the right choice. Here again, we were very much helped by our Consultants, who between them knew intimately every scientific area in which we were interested and, in many cases, had a first-hand knowledge of a candidate's work. We were often able to make direct approaches through one of them to men we wanted and as a result the rapid increase in our scientific staff did not take place at the expense of quality.

With the increase of our reputation as marketeers we came up against a particular problem which we never solved. Just as young ambitious chemists sought a job with I.C.I., knowing that this background and the training would help them land top appointments elsewhere later on, so young marketing men sought employment with the British subsidiary of Procter & Gamble, the great U.S. company, so as to get a U.S. marketing training. As our reputation increased, young men turned to

Beechams with the same objective and we found that many of our best young men marched out into top jobs before we could ourselves promote them. We had always paid well and had aimed to maintain conditions of service in excess of the 'market' both in our factories and in our executive echelons. This did not deal with this particular problem. Young men took no notice of the fact that we were paying up to 20 per cent of their annual salary as premiums for their 'top hat' pensions: retirement was a long way off. Furthermore, the salaries for the jobs they went to were set at what had to be paid to get them. The Managing Director of Aspro-Nicholas once boasted to me that he could, and would, buy anyone he wanted from Beechams, simply by offering a salary 50 per cent higher than they were getting from us! He was an Australian and like many of his countrymen inclined to exaggerate but undoubtedly he could and, in fact, did buy a number of our men.

So we had to do the best we could to improve our management, in a variety of ways, but it always remained the factor limiting our growth right up to the time of my retirement. I was probably the wrong type of leader to solve this problem and I believe that my successor, Sir Ronald Edwards, made a better job of it. I can only claim to have left such men of high calibre as Bob Wilkins, Ronnie Halstead, Bill Petley, Jim Sullivan, and Frank Lomax; but they all blossomed under Sir Ronald and certainly fought their own way up from the early days without any noticeable help from me.

This then was the position as we moved into 1963 and I must now go back and deal with the commercial development of our new penicillins and its momentous effect on Beechams.

14 *Commercial Development of the New Penicillins*

With the signing of the Bristol-Myers agreement in April 1959 we addressed ourselves to the commercial development of our discoveries. By that time we had produced over 200 new penicillins and, coinciding with an annotation in the *Lancet*, we called a press conference on 6 March 1959. This achieved world-wide notice in the press and on radio and television. The team of young scientists responsible came in for much attention and particular interest was shown in their youth. Peter Doyle was 37, George Rolinson 32, John Nayler 31, and Ralph Batchelor 27.

The discovery also marked the beginning of Ernst Chain's period of triumphant recognition in Britain and the expansion of his worldwide fame. He was to take up the Chair of Biochemistry at Imperial College, London, receive a Knighthood, and many other honours. Admittedly, he had not predicted the form of our discovery but he had led us to continue research on penicillin and it was by following the paths he had indicated that the observation was made. Furthermore, he had accurately prophesied what we should subsequently achieve. He said that he would expect us to find penicillins completely different from G and V, with a very broad spectrum of activity; that we should also find penicillins resistant to penicillinase, an enzyme produced by certain bacteria, which inactivates the penicillins G and V by breaking down their molecular structure. If we could make new penicillins with side chains more firmly attached so as to resist this breakdown we should be able to deal with the so-called resistant staphylococci, those lethal penicillinase producing bacteria which were infecting so many hospitals and maternity homes and killing patients and babies.

He also expressed the belief that we should be able to produce penicillins that were non-allergenic. We have, in fact, achieved all but the last prediction, although here we have increased our knowledge greatly and have also much reduced the likelihood of allergic reactions.

Included in the first 200 new penicillins we made were two very important compounds. One appeared to have a broad spectrum, being active against a very wide range of bacteria. The other killed a fairly wide range of bacteria and was entirely stable in the presence of penicillinase, the substance which destroyed penicillin and which was secreted by the so-called 'resistant' bacteria. Thus, for the first time, we would be able to deal with bacteria immune to penicillin and in many cases any other antibiotic. Research effort was therefore concentrated on these two compounds. Besides pursuing all the laboratory tests necessary we had to study how to make the compounds in volume at a reasonable cost. The broad-spectrum compound was particularly difficult and Bristol-Myers at first took no interest in it because they felt that it could never be produced economically.

It was imperative that we should concentrate our pharmaceutical management under the most appropriate men we had on our staff. In September 1959 Beecham Research Laboratories Ltd., which up to then had been the company responsible for research, assumed commercial responsibility for all our ethical pharmaceutical business worldwide and we merged C. L. Bencard Ltd. with it. We chose to operate under the name Beecham Research Laboratories because it had received worldwide publicity. Douglas Stafford became the Managing Director of the combined business. He had for years been reminding me that he could not meet my demands for growth in C. L. Bencard Ltd. (up to this time our only ethical pharmaceutical business) until something came out of research. Now he had more than he bargained for! The penicillin discovery not only changed Beechams, but also the lives of many Beecham employees, and none more so than Doug. He became the Chief Executive of this new division with infinite opportunities, and we were very fortunate to have available a man who measured up to the challenge.

First of all I gave him *carte blanche* with the commercial organization, charged him to build it up quickly, and in particular to develop a powerful detail force. I told him that he could have anyone he wished transferred to his division and here he first revealed his shrewd judgment of men. He chose as his Assistant Managing Director Bob Wilkins, who was at that time a Vice-President of Beecham Inc. (U.S.A.), responsible for South America. Before that Bob, who was a chemist, had been Technical Director for the Western Hemisphere. This was the key appointment and Bob soon showed that he was made for the job. Imperturbable, with a fine scientific mind that also comprehended marketing, he was liked and respected by everyone he dealt with. Then Doug asked for Ronnie Halstead, whose career has already been summarized in Chapter 11. Doug's next choice was Frank Lomax, another chemist who had started with us in the Macleans factory, transferred to Eire as factory manager, and then assumed the office of Managing Director of the Irish company. Frank was a surprise choice for Export Director and again vindicated Doug's judgment. Finally, technical men were drawn from around the Group and we built up a fine team to run the Worthing factory, some of whom went to Bristol Laboratories at Syracuse, New York State, for indoctrination into the techniques of fermentation chemistry.

In September 1959 Bristol-Myers advised us that they were going to market a phenoxy-ethyl compound produced by them, which was quite easy to manufacture by a straight chemical reaction on a purified fermentation broth and which had certain qualities which made it superior to penicillin V. We arranged with Bristol to supply us in bulk with the compound and in November launched our first new penicillin under the brand Broxil.

Then on 2 September 1960 we launched Celbenin (methicillin) our penicillinase-resistant compound. It was not stable in acid, which meant that it had to be given by injection and this called for sterile areas for manufacturing and packaging. The latter were converted at the Macleans factory and were all we had until our Worthing facilities became available. Celbenin's activity was not as high as we would have wished and we were developing other compounds which were likely to show greater activity and also be capable of oral administration. However, the need for it was urgent. In hospitals all over the country the menace of the resistant staphylococci was growing. Patients admitted for entirely different diseases were getting intractable staphylococcal infections, most of them serious and many fatal. In hospitals where penicillin G had been widely used whole wards had to be closed because they had been colonized by strains of bacteria which were impervious to the penicillins then available, or for that matter, any other antibiotic. In some hospitals 80 per cent of the staphylococci found there belonged to the resistant strains.

The appearance of Celbenin was therefore an event of outstanding importance. Many papers on it appeared in the medical journals and demand came from all over the world. However, whilst it made our reputation it was not going to make our fortune, because its use cleared up resistant staphylococcal infections in the hospitals and thereafter it was in demand only to deal with sporadic outbreaks.

Thus we entered the financial year 1960–61 with the new Beecham Research Laboratories in operation and immersed in negotiations for marketing our developing compounds all over the world. It would take time to develop our own overseas pharmaceutical organization so that meanwhile we had to make adequate licensing arrangements which left us free to enter the markets ourselves in due course. Sales and royalties were, of course, still on a modest scale, research expenditure was rising fast as I had taken my foot off the brake, and the Division was losing money.

All this time work had been proceeding on our broad-spectrum compound (ampicillin) which we were planning to put out under the trade mark Penbritin. It was becoming clear that this was an outstanding broad-spectrum antibiotic which could be used with safety in high dosage. However, it was very difficult to make and we had many problems to overcome before it could be manufactured at a reasonable cost. Indeed, in the early days it had been contended that we would never be able to manufacture it economically. Our scientists persevered and finally determined that our cheapest method of production was to split 6-amino-penicillanic acid (6-APA) from penicillin G by means of a process invented by Bayer A.G. of Germany and then to attach the side chain to 6-APA by chemical means. Costs were still very high but we were able to produce reasonable quantities and on 21 July 1961 made supplies available to hospitals.

Broad-spectrum antibiotics by their very nature made up over 50 per cent of the total antibiotic market. They were used in the treatment of a wide range of bacterial infections such as pneumonia, bronchitis, and urinary tract infections. Our principal competitors were Parke-Davis' Chloramphenicol and Pfizer's Tetracycline and we set our price at double that of the latter. At the time of our launch our selling price was less than our cost of production, but we were confident by that time that we would be able to achieve progressive cost reductions.

Chloramphenicol had a serious side effect and Penbritin would certainly supplant it for everything but the treatment of typhoid. Even in this case Penbritin could be used to deal with typhoid carriers because it could be administered in massive dosage. Its big advantage over the tetracyclines was that Penbritin was bactericidal (it killed bacteria) whereas the tetracyclines were bacteriostatic (they held bacteria in suspense until they died).

Because of production difficulties we had to move slowly with Penbritin. It was not until the second half of 1963 that we could make supplies generally available and commence our intensive worldwide marketing campaign. Results were phenomenal. Sales of Penbritin very quickly outstripped those of our famous advertised proprietaries to become our biggest selling brand.

The period 1961–69 was probably the most hectic in the whole history of the Group. During that time our pharmaceutical sales rose from £2·8 million to £32·8 million; we continued to expand at Worthing until we could go no further there and in 1970 had to look to Scotland for a second factory; we erected a factory at Piscataway in the U.S.A. and started on plans for a factory at Heppignies in Belgium and one at Singapore. Research was expanded at a great rate and in the financial year 1968–69 we were spending £2·3 million compared with £521,000 in 1961–62. We had acquired Vitamins Ltd., which broadened our base in the agricultural and veterinary fields and presented us with another research station at Walton Oaks.

At the same time we had to maintain a continuous dialogue with the Ministry of Health over prices. Our top management was also very much taken up with the Sainsbury Committee of Enquiry into the relationship of the pharmaceutical industry with the National Health Service. This Committee was set up by the Socialist Government and chaired by a Socialist who I knew had no belief in advertising or proprietary branded products. I felt it to be a great threat to our future and we did our best to educate the Committee in some of the facts of life.

Whilst all this was going on we were launching three new penicillins. In October 1962 there was Orbenin (cloxacillin), which gave us a much better compound for dealing with the resistant staphylococci. It achieved higher blood levels and was capable also of being taken by mouth. It could also be combined with Penbritin (ampicillin) so as to provide a product with a very broad spectrum of activity. We sold this combination as Ampliclox and I have personal knowledge of its life-saving qualities. Then in 1967 we launched Pyopen (carbenicillin), the first penicillin to deal with killer infections to which seriously ill patients are specially vulnerable. Other compounds have been put on the market since my retirement including one which could prove superior to Penbritin.

Time and the market place have established the tremendous importance of our discovery. The use of the new penicillins is still increasing throughout the world and the benefits to mankind have already been inestimable. It seems to me that we shall long continue to rely on them to cure many of our ills.

15 *Europe*

When John Buckley dismissed Gordon Dunbar in 1951 he broke up Beecham Export Corporation and allowed Macleans, County Perfumery, St Helens, and Eno to control their export business and their overseas subsidiaries and factories. As I have mentioned, on taking over as Chief Executive I took personal responsibility for the Western Hemisphere, leaving the rest of the world to continue to be controlled by the individual companies. This was not because I thought it would get us anywhere but because I did not want to alter too much at one time, and certainly not before we had found and pulled out a capable overseas executive staff. Then on the break-up of the Watford Group in 1953 we decided to centralize control of all overseas business other than the Western Hemisphere under the Beecham Overseas Department at Headquarters (later to become Beecham Overseas Ltd.) which was the responsibility of John Rintoul. At that time in Europe we were served mainly by selling agents and goods were exported there, except in the case of Denmark, where Macleans had a factory, and France, where Eno had one.

Our French business was very small and based almost entirely on Eno's. France was a very difficult market for proprietary products because the pharmacist had a legal monopoly and, in addition, Government interfered by means of price control and in many other ways. West Germany was a closed book. In company with a great many British businesses, Beechams had made no effort to enter Germany after the war. Feeling towards the Germans was too bitter, and we were to pay for our neglect. The Americans moved in and undoubtedly gained substantial advantage from their early start.

County Laboratories had made some effort to build a business in Italy and in 1953 appointed Joe Nissim as their selling agent.

Joe was a remarkable man. Of Greek birth, he had fought in the British Army during the war and afterwards moved to Italy, leaving one brother behind in Greece and sending another one to open up an agency business in France. Italy was very backward in the marketing sense. Advertising expenditure was low, there was no television, and very few good advertising agencies. Supermarkets were almost non-existent and proprietary products were sold through over 100,000 small shops. This called for a large, expensive sales force. Joe Nissim obtained the sales agency for Procter & Gamble of the U.S.A., selling their detergents and soaps, and he went to America for training and indoctrination. He had built up a very large and powerful sales force, supported by an I.B.M. computer, I would guess one of the first in Italy, and certainly he had one before Beechams. He did not want to rely entirely on Procter & Gamble and therefore he approached Beechams and we negotiated a complex agreement with him for the manufacture and marketing of Beecham proprietary brands in Italy. It was in the early part of 1957 that we entered into this new arrangement which resulted in outstanding success in selling shampoos but only modest success with Brylcreem and Macleans Tooth Paste. For most of the time we were arguing with Joe over our agreement, which we felt gave him most of the profits. Various amendments were made and in 1968 we agreed to set up a jointly owned company. He certainly played his cards superbly and managed to remain on terms with both Procter & Gamble and Beechams whilst acquiring other businesses himself to provide further products for his sales forces (in due course he had split his original sales force into two).

With our commitments in the U.S.A. I did not want Beechams to become involved in heavy development in a major market until it was clear that the U.S.A. was capable of yielding a reasonable profit. Therefore we did nothing in Germany and France and concentrated on building up our businesses in the smaller countries. We were reasonably successful in Belgium, Holland, and Denmark in which latter country, as mentioned elsewhere, we held over 30 per cent of the tooth paste market at one time. By 1956 local companies had been formed in these

three territories and we proceeded to acquire factories in
Holland and Belgium and employ our own sales forces. With
all this development, profits were very low. In 1956–57, for
instance, Belgium, Denmark, and Holland yielded only £23,000
profit and France lost £3,000. This compared with profits of
£164,000 in South Africa and Rhodesia!

Then in 1964–65 a substantial profit accrued in the U.S.A.
and we were able to give serious consideration to our European
proprietary business. I commissioned Booz Allen & Hamilton
to make a survey of possible French and German businesses
which might be acquired. It was easy to pick out the businesses
we would like to buy but not so easy to get them. The Americans had been around long before us and had snapped up
those companies which were available, paying very high prices.
Our experience in Italy and in the smaller markets convinced
me that we had to acquire an established business before we
could really attack either Germany or France. This would not
avoid development losses but they would not be so heavy as if
we had started from scratch, nor would it take so long. Furthermore, if we could get a well-run business we would have a
local executive to work with. This was important, not the least
because starting from scratch was perhaps the most difficult of
all operations and called for the highest calibre of executive.
Booz Allen put their finger on some businesses but we could
not persuade the proprietors to sell. However, in 1964 I was
approached by a man I had met in connection with my work
for the British Heart Foundation Appeal. He introduced me to
Mr Karl Brixner, a German financier who was an associate
of Helmut Schroeder, Chairman and a minority shareholder of
Blendax A.G., a German company marketing a number of
proprietary products but principally Blendax and Blend-a-med
tooth pastes. Blend-a-med was promoted for pyorrhoea, but
Blendax was heavily advertised and looked as if it had been
based on Macleans. The formula was different but the flavour,
the pack, and the claims were similar.

I and some of our executive had a few meetings with Mr
Brixner and Mr Schroeder and visited the factories and offices
in the Frankfurt area. Blendax was locked in deadly combat

with Colgate and we were told that Schroeder recognized that they needed more strength and ought to merge with an international company. Apparently the family that owned the vast majority of the shares needed to be persuaded, and in the meantime Schroeder offered us, firstly, sole rights to the Blendax overseas business and trade marks (this was small) and a majority interest in Margaret Astor. This company was associated with Blendax but here Schroeder had control. It sold a range of popular cosmetics and was one of the biggest cosmetic houses in Germany. We had been looking at the cosmetic business for some time. A number of advertised proprietary categories had first appeared as part of the various cosmetic ranges. Lipsticks, nail varnishes, hair sprays, and eye make-up were now clearly in the advertised proprietary business and I felt that there was a strong case for our entering at least the decorative end of the cosmetic field. So after long negotiations we made an agreement with Schroeder and his associates, taking a 51 per cent interest in Margaret Astor, with various options which would in due course entitle us to take up the rest of the shares.

Then in 1966 we learnt that Schroeder and the Blendax family had fallen out, and that he had left the business. We had several meetings with family representatives but it became clear that they were not prepared to sell and so we turned to the development of Margaret Astor. We acquired a further 24 per cent of the shares in 1965 and were able to purchase the remainder in 1967.

Helmut Schroeder had a son, Juergen, and we formed a high opinion of him. He had spent two years in the U.S.A. working for Coty, and was used to operating in a big company. His English was perfect and he got on well with all our executives. In due course we made him Chief Executive of the business. It was very successful, gaining 30 per cent of the lipstick market, 20 per cent of the eye make-up market, and 20 per cent of the nail varnish market. By 1970 sales had more than doubled to over £5 million and profits had increased from a mere £40,000 to £900,000 per annum. However, this did not solve our big problem of finding a base on which to build our proprietary business and in Germany we had to keep looking for an opportunity. This has now appeared in the business of Fischer & Fischer (Badedas), purchased in 1970 after my retirement.

In 1966 we learnt that M. Georges Wurz was ready to sell his cosmetic business named Lancaster, which was based in Monaco, and we made contact with him. He had been approached by Americans but we understood he was loath to sell to them. Anyway, it was necessary to get French approval to a sale and the Americans were out of favour. We quickly agreed terms and were able to get the approval of the French Ministry of Finance, subject to conditions. The business was named after the Lancaster bombers which had night after night droned over France and had become a household word there. Wurz commenced operations soon after the war in partnership with his brother and a chemist associate from premises in Monte Carlo. They concentrated their efforts on establishing a substantial business in France. Lancaster products were high class and expensive, and were marketed through exclusive retailers. They were aimed at the middle-aged woman to 'halt the march of time' (*arrête la marche du temps*). Some of the claims made were pretty strong and caused eyebrows to be raised at home and in the U.S.A. Anyway, the products were very good and the business had been fantastically successful. In due course the brother had moved to San Remo and had achieved wonderful sales in Italy where Lancaster was the best selling high-class cosmetic line.

George Wurz wished to retire but agreed to remain as Chairman whilst his son, Jean-Pierre, established himself as the Chief Executive. This was gambling again on a son being able to follow in his father's footsteps and, again, the gamble appears to have succeeded. The business has continued to grow and has now opened up in Germany. When we came on the scene in 1966 total sales were £1,400,000 and profits £205,000. In 1970 sales were £3,372,000 and profits £556,000.

Beechams have not yet tackled the French proprietary market which I believe to be the toughest of all. I think that it is essential to acquire the right business before attempting such a move, and even then I would not make the assumption that products successful elsewhere could necessarily be marketed in France.

The headquarters control of Europe from 1953 to 1967 rested in various hands. First, as part of Beecham Overseas Ltd. it was overseen by John Rintoul with Tony Fabricius as Managing Director and Ted Godden as his assistant. Then Tony Fabricius became Chairman of Beecham Toiletry Division with Ted Godden as his European Director. In January 1967 Ken Moore assumed the Chairmanship of European Division, with Godden as his Vice-Chairman. Developing our proprietary brands in the major countries of Europe called for marketing abilities of a high order. Looking back it seems to me that at no time was management adequate for the task it faced until January 1968. On that date Doug Stafford assumed overall responsibility for all our business in Europe, both pharmaceutical and proprietary, with Frank Lomax as his Vice-Chairman. Doug was also Executive Vice-Chairman of the Group and the main burden of Europe fell on Frank's deceptively bowed but broad and strong shoulders.

Frank Lomax was one of the men given a great opportunity by the Beecham penicillin discovery. He started life in the Macleans factory as a chemist. Then he was transferred to Eire to run the factory there and progressed to control the Irish company. When I offered Doug his pick of the Group's executives to set up the new pharmaceutical company, one of the men he chose, to my surprise, was Frank Lomax. Doug was a fine 'picker' and in Frank he put his finger on a man with great potential. A tremendous worker of spartan integrity (I used to call him Oliver Cromwell), he drove himself to the limit of endurance, and travelled more than 100,000 air miles a year in his ceaseless drive to build up the new Pharmaceutical Division's overseas business. Then when I asked Doug to become responsible for Europe and to undertake what would be his last great service to the Group, he again asked for Frank Lomax as his Chief Executive.

In 1967–68 sales in Europe were £14·2 million and profits £2·3 million. In 1971–72 sales were £48·6 million, profits were £10·8 million, and royalties yielded £2·5 million. This was not bad going for such a short period. Europe is now a major factor in the Group's business and contributes more profit than the Western Hemisphere. Cosmetics have done well, but proprietaries have still to be established as a major factor. The main effort has so far taken place in the pharmaceutical field, and here considerable progress has been made.

When Beechams made its famous discovery we had practically no pharmaceutical business in Europe. C. L. Bencard Ltd. had a sales agent in Belgium for its allergy injections and one in Holland for Ferraplex B, an iron vitamin compound. Both these agents were given some new penicillins to sell. Manufacturing licences were given to Bayer in Germany (in exchange for the penicillin G splitting process), to Astra in Scandinavia, and to Farmitalia in Italy. Selling licensees were then appointed in other countries, notably Delagrange in France and Bonet in Spain.

Generally speaking, progress was unsatisfactory through agents and we had to pursue as quickly as possible our firm policy, announced to all licensees right at the start, of establishing our own marketing organization in all countries. Europe is a very complex organism in spite of the Common Market. Government registration procedures for new drugs are specific to each territory and are yearly becoming more complex and more expensive to comply with. Every European health service has different rules and lengthy negotiations with authorities, that can take a year or more, have to be undertaken in almost all markets. There are many pending E.E.C. directives to harmonize national regulations, but little progress has been made in practical terms.

Our progress in building up our own marketing organization turned on our ability to recruit able nationals. We were fortunate in Holland where Mr B. Verburgh was managing the business of our agent there. He impressed us with his ability and in due course joined us when we formed our own company in 1967. It was very successful and Beechams now have 40 per cent of the broad-spectrum antibiotic market in Holland. Mr Verburgh was made a Director of Beecham Pharmaceuticals and controlled the whole of our European pharmaceutical business.

Over the years we have built up an able team, but it is still necessary to have ability in every territory as a scrutiny of the territorial sales and profits figures will demonstrate. For example, in Spain Mr F. Bonet had been our agent for Eno's 'Fruit Salt' since 1924. He had always done a good job and it is worth recording that today *per capita* sales of Eno's in Spain are the second highest in the world. When the discovery was made, Bonet asked for a licence to promote Beecham penicillins in Spain. We were not very enthusiastic and anyway it was difficult in those days to open up new business in Spain. However, by 1966 we had obtained official approval and made arrangements for his company to process our compounds and sell them. Frank Lomax believed that the key to success was a detail force trained by us. He therefore ran a test, leaving Bonet to market our products in Madrid while a Beecham-trained detail force operated in Barcelona. After nine months, results were conclusive and Bonet asked us to train and control his detail force. This has now grown to 120 men (our largest force in Europe) and sales are in excess of £7 million per annum.

Medical representatives are the spearheads of pharmaceutical marketing and on the continent of Europe these were usually pharmacists, failed medical students, and even doctors. Beechams broke with this tradition and looked for men of personality and intelligence who could be trained to become highly expert in our field of pharmaceutical knowledge. We then organized their day so that they concentrated on the most important doctors in general practice and in hospitals. Medical practice in the use of antibiotics varies enormously in different parts of Europe. Some countries favour combinations of drugs, others prefer to inject, and in France, for instance, the administration of antibiotics by means of suppositories is popular. All this had to be taken into account by our marketing teams and it was impossible to apply one standard approach to Europe.

I do not propose to describe our efforts country by country. Every one was different and presented us with its own unique problems. Only Germany gave us a really difficult time, due mainly to the fact that Bayer had a licence from us and they dominated the hospitals where 40 per cent of all antibiotics were used. This compared with 20 per cent in England. We found it very difficult to make any progress with Penbritin, our big seller everywhere else, and only when we launched our new compound Carbenicillin were we able to get a toe-hold in the market. Now compounds are coming along to which Bayer have no rights and I have no doubt that this will enable Beechams to make substantial progress. The team there has been tempered in a fire of adversity and will be all the better for it when things get easier.

Looking at the figures for Europe one can legitimately ask what would the position be today had we made our effort there at an earlier date, say 1960, and held back in the U.S.A.? I personally do not think that we could have gone much faster in the pharmaceutical field, but would we by now have a bigger share of the proprietary market? It really all turns on whether we could have found more companies to build on had we started to look earlier, and perhaps this is where I made my big mistake. If I had my time over again I would still have made the effort in the U.S.A. but I would have looked earlier and harder for acquisitions in Europe, despite the fact that we could not have spent much development money there before we did.

However, it is never too late and Beechams is now poised for big things in Europe. It is fast building a fine pharmaceutical presence. Its cosmetics are well established and the company have the know-how to develop this business all over the world. Finally, there is now the muscle to build a proprietary business and there is acquired marketing experience in the U.S.A. and the U.K. to ensure that the job is done properly.

16 *Beecham Inc.*

In 1964, when Maurice Bale returned to the U.S.A. as President of Beecham Products Inc., Australia and New Zealand were added to what we then called the Western Hemisphere Division. I arranged this partly because Australia was very much influenced by U.S. practices. Most of the big U.S. proprietary companies had subsidiaries there run by Americans transferred from the U.S.A. and I felt that direct U.S. influence would help our business, which had not achieved much growth in recent years.

I was also thinking of the day when we would want to set up a U.S. company which could raise money by issuing shares on the New York Stock Exchange. We were already planning to build a U.S. pharmaceutical factory and this would call for substantial capital. Furthermore, I was turning my mind more and more to speeding our growth by acquisition and in the U.S.A. this meant that we had to be flexible. The U.S.A. had a capital gains tax which took 25 per cent of all capital profits. Thus when proprietors sold their shares for cash they were liable to capital gains tax but if they could exchange their shares for shares in another company they would not be liable, unless and until the shares in that company were sold. Then, of course, Beechams could not remit cash to finance its business in the U.S.A. except through the dollar premium account at a very high penalty. This was before the sophisticated procedures of the Eurodollar market had been developed. I felt that in due course we could set up a company in the U.S.A. owning and controlling our businesses in Canada, the whole of South America, Australia, and New Zealand. The Far East might also be included as I thought that Australia was the best place to have a sub-group to control the whole of that area. Such a company could issue shares on the market and provided

Beechams retained sufficient for control this would enable us to use paper as part of a purchase price. Finally, as we grew— and I was still dreaming of that great U.S. company bigger than the rest of Beechams – we would be able to start creating the fund of shares 'in Treasury'. This is a very convenient procedure, not permitted by British company law, which enables U.S. companies to buy up their own stock on the market and carry it on their books for subsequent re-issue. Quite often such shares are used in payment or part-payment for an acquisition, or in respect of stock options given to executives. I was thinking primarily of acquisitions.

Our pharmaceutical business was growing fast and there were unlimited opportunities in the proprietary field not only in the U.S.A. but in the rest of the territory in which companies controlled by Beecham Products Inc. operated. It seemed to me at that time that Beecham Group was approaching a period when substantial profits would accrue from pharmaceuticals and that during such a period some of those profits could be used in the U.S.A. and elsewhere to develop our proprietary business to its maximum extent. We could establish tooth paste worldwide and then develop our shampoos and deodorants. Brylcreem had already been widely promoted.

Meanwhile, I made two attempts to acquire businesses, offering either cash or Beecham Group shares, or shares in a new U.S. company, or a mixture. Early in 1965 I approached Mr Burns of the U.S. Vitamin Corporation. This was a small U.S. 'ethical' drug company operating out of New York. They specialized in vitamin products and, as a matter of deliberate, policy kept away from the big markets and from head-on competition with the big companies. I thought that they were interested at first, but nothing came of the meetings. I made it clear that I should expect to build our U.S. pharmaceutical business on their company and management, and maybe they did not relish the idea of slugging it out with the big U.S. antibiotic houses.

Then in September 1965 I approached Mr Frank DeFriece Jnr., the Chairman and Chief Executive of the S. E. Massengill Co. of Bristol, Tennessee. Massengill had some good proprietary products which were advertised and sold direct to the public and a reasonable catalogue of medicines for prescription by doctors, but with nothing outstanding. However, they had a medical detail force of over 200 men and I felt that we could give them plenty to sell. I knew that they had been approached by some of the big U.S. companies and again I offered the alternatives and again made it clear that I wanted to build on them. Again I failed to convince, and Frank and his family decided to go to the market to raise the money they wanted. Subsequently, of course, we came together but that was in 1970 while I was still Chairman of Beecham Inc. but after I had retired as Chairman of Beechams.

Having failed to acquire a company on which we could build our U.S. pharmaceutical business, matters came to a head towards the end of 1967. We had to decide on future management and how we were going to pay for the antibiotic factory to which we had finally committed ourselves. Up to that time the Beecham Products Inc. executive had not been responsible for pharmaceuticals, but they had been drawn more and more into the interminable arguments between the Pharmaceutical Division back in Britain and Ayerst Laboratories, who were Beechams' partners in a joint company to market our new penicillins in the U.S.A. I came to the conclusion that it was time we had a strong pharmaceutical management on the spot, and we finally took the decision to set up the U.S. company of my dreams by transferring ownership of all Beechams business, both proprietary and pharmaceutical, in Australia, New Zealand, South America, and Canada to a new U.S. company and to offer 10 per cent of that company's shares on the New York curb exchange. In this we were advised by Stanley Miller of Goldman Sachs of Wall Street. I had asked Goldman Sachs for advice when I made my first approach to Frank DeFriece of Massengill in 1965 and Stanley had accompanied me when I had visited Frank at Bristol, Tennessee. Stanley's idea was that we could move on to the New York Stock Exchange at a later date, when more shares were available to the public, either as a result of a merger or if and when we needed additional capital as a result of internal growth.

	Fiscal year ended March 31,				
	1968	1967	1966	1965	1964
	(thousands of dollars)				
Net sales	$66,345	$56,598	$47,570	$38,723	$29,799
Other income	485	605	578	475	355
	66,830	57,203	48,148	39,198	30,154
Costs and expenses:					
Cost of goods sold	21,435	17,659	14,866	12,312	9,552
Selling and administrative	35,514	30,880	26,487	22,971	18,779
Other charges—interest and exchange loss	194	139	191	201	298
Minority interest	56	232	56	(559)	(125)
	57,199	48,910	41,600	34,925	28,504
Income from operations before federal income taxes and extraordinary items	9,631	8,293	6,548	4,273	1,650
Provision for income taxes before application of operating loss carryforwards:					
United States	2,864	2,636	2,016	1,358	(31)
Foreign	1,754	1,389	1,024	1,022	957
	4,618	4,025	3,040	2,380	926
Income before extraordinary items	5,013	4,268	3,508	1,893	724
Loss on sale of Mexican plant					(114)
Credits arising from utilization of operating loss carryforwards	54	227	55		
Net income	$ 5,067	$ 4,495	$ 3,563	$ 1,893	$ 610
Per shaae of common stock:					
Income before extraordinary items	$ 1.39	$ 1.19	$ .97	$ .53	$ .20
Extraordinary items	.02	.06	.02		(.03)
Net income	$ 1.41	$ 1.25	$ .99	$ .53	$ .17

Our Prospectus was in the standard U.S. form and provided a potted history of the business we had to offer. The main figures are shown on the previous page.

By this means we sold 400,000 shares of Common Stock at $28 per share which, after expenses, yielded us $10,600,000. Approximately $7,000,000 was needed to pay for the new antibiotic factory built at Piscataway and its first extension.

This move did not solve our U.S. management problems – it made them infinitely worse, because I had now overtaxed Maurice Bale, who as President was responsible for the whole business. He had lost Ronnie Halstead who had been recalled to England to join the Board and take charge first of the Food and Drink Division and, subsequently, of the Products Division when we combined all our proprietary business under one management team. Maurice was fascinated by the pharmaceutical business but he knew little about it and was badly served on the technical side. On top of this I had dumped into his lap problems of which I was unaware. There can be no doubt that we badly underestimated the technical difficulties in setting up a new plant abroad, and we did not provide adequate supervision from England. Our troubles were compounded by the need for speed when at last we got underway. Ayerst were clearly not ready to take the risks that we were. Alvin Brush, who was then the Chairman and Chief Executive of American Home Products, the parent company of Ayerst, had been very careful to keep his group's antibiotic manufacturing capacity below the market demand. Their policy appeared to be to run their own plant flat out and purchase the balance of their requirements on the market. He took a similar view in regard to our business and was loath to agree to providing half the capital to build a plant capable of producing considerably more than we were then selling.

Our position was very difficult. We were manufacturing Ampicillin in rented facilities at one factory, filling sterile injectable products in another factory, and packing in a third. Thanks to the remarkable efforts of Colin West, a scientist who had been employed at our Worthing factory and who had then joined us in the U.S.A., we had maintained a surprisingly high standard but it could not go on and the U.S. Food and Drug Administration were becoming restive. I had been impressed by Alvin Brush's reasoning and had counselled Doug Stafford to have patience. However, Doug became desperate in his representations and I finally agreed that Beechams would go it alone and build the factory at its own expense and on its own authority. This was a big decision which necessitated a renegotiation of our agreement with Ayerst. However, time was running out: we were warned by the Authorities that they would not allow us to continue our present arrangements for much longer, and so when Colin West came to us with a new factory, built by speculators on a fine piece of land of adequate size to take care of all foreseeable expansion and with adequate provision for effluent, we agreed to its purchase. The building was merely a shell and it still took some time to convert it to our requirements and to assemble the plant. Our haste to get all this done was to have serious consequences later on. In the event we got into production in June 1967 and for a time all went well, but then all sorts of troubles hit us, the most serious of which was periodic failure to maintain sterility in our sterile areas. It transpired that we had in some cases installed plant and equipment which was different from that used in England and therefore it was impossible just to copy British practices. To add to our difficulties, there was a conspiracy of silence which kept the true facts from us and I was left to realize from the figures that there must be greater trouble than was admitted. Our costs were much too high, and I did not believe that this was all due to low throughput as was represented to me.

On top of our pharmaceutical problems our proprietary marketing team had changed and was poor, and we were ill equipped to withstand the storms that blew up in both the hairdressing and dentifrice markets. In hair dressings (helped, I believe, by all the knocking copy indulged in by the competing brands) the public turned away from traditional products. The younger generation either used nothing, or the new hair sprays which were appearing in large numbers. In the dentifrice market Macleans had woken things up with a vengeance and new brands, new flavours, and new fluoride pastes continued to appear, all being launched by means of massive sampling campaigns and heavy advertising.

Then some of our charming competitors encouraged attacks on abrasive tooth pastes. The American Dental Association finally got into the act and in due course published some figures relating to all the popular tooth pastes which amusingly put one of our competitors, who I believed encouraged the attack, high on the list for high abrasion; we were about midway. In my opinion, the whole thing was nonsense. First of all, one had to define what one meant by 'abrasion'. Dental plaque is what a tooth paste is made to remove from the teeth, and in one sense this has to be 'abraded' if it is to come off. The tests used by some authorities consisted of rubbing extracted teeth with tooth paste for days on end and this was then related to years of usage twice a day for a given number of minutes. But in practice teeth are brushed for a few minutes night and morning and during this time plaque and other debris is being removed. The plaque forms again every day and so one seldom in fact rubs on a clean surface – never, if the tooth paste is not sufficiently abrasive to remove any plaque. Macleans Tooth Paste was based on special chalks which were free of silica and it had a unique ability to clean teeth effectively. We were thus justified in our claim that Macleans made teeth whiter as we could show that it *was* superior in this respect. There has never been any evidence that it will scratch teeth or cause any more wear than the wrong use of a tooth brush will do on its own. We needed steady nerves to cope with the situation created by all the furore, and these were noticeable by their absence.

Our Western Hemisphere business is now under the firm control of Bill Petley, who was appointed President of Beecham Inc. on 1 April 1971. The Beecham and Massengill businesses were merged in August 1971 and at that time we decided to wind-up our U.S. public company, Beecham Inc., and pay off the outside shareholders, because had it remained as a U.S. public company, goodwill arising on the acquisition would have had to be written off against its net income. Whilst this was a valid reason it was clear that neither Sir Ronald Edwards nor the other executive directors were so besotted with the U.S.A. as I was, and certainly they were not dreaming my old dreams of a U.S. company bigger than the parent.

Bill Petley has had a remarkable career with Beechams and with Bob Wilkins and Ronnie Halstead can be held up as examples of how men of great ability can be encouraged and fostered in a company, *provided* one is prepared to make a way for them to move up and to protect them from enemies on the way. Bill started life with us as an accountant. He was an abrasive personality and could not hide his contempt for lesser intellects who were his peers or superiors. On the other hand, he always supported people responsible to him. He first demonstrated his outstanding ability when he conducted negotiations on behalf of the Pharmaceutical Division with the Ministry of Health over prices. Had I listened to Philippa Lane, at that time our Personnel Director, I would have appointed him Financial Director on the death of Mike Spry, but he landed the job in January 1967 and within a matter of months it was revealed that Beechams had got a Financial Director of outstanding ability and iron nerve. He was invaluable to my successor when he took over, and when we entered into negotiations again with Frank DeFriece for the acquisition of Massengill, it was Bill who acted on our behalf in the negotiations. I witnessed some of these discussions and later on heard Frank's paean of praise for Bill, and it suddenly dawned on me that here was the answer to our U.S. problems. As a result I recommended to Sir Ronald that he make Bill Petley the U.S. Chief Executive and I am glad to say that he agreed. I believe that this will put to rights the mess I left him in the Pharmaceutical Division when I retired from the Chairmanship of the U.S. Company in March 1972.

The U.S. market is not one for softies to tackle. It is tough and ruthless and one can never sit back and relax. This is particularly true of the big segments like antibiotics and toiletries. Anything goes here, and one has to wage war on two fronts: with one's competitors and with the authorities. I hope that Bill will return to the attack on the toiletry market.

There is still an opportunity for Macleans Tooth Paste. Brylcreem will come back again and then we have the cosmetics and deodorants which have not yet been tackled. Added to all this we have the very fine Massengill products for feminine hygiene. It is bound to be tough but the rewards are very great, not only because the U.S.A. is an immense market but because of its influence overseas.

I do not believe that one can establish a worldwide brand unless it is firmly established in the U.S.A. This view of mine can be debated at length, but I can mention a few reasons for my belief. Firstly, success in the U.S.A. proves that the product is good enough to withstand U.S. competition anywhere else, and in our markets it is U.S. competition that counts. It also proves the marketing approach. Then there is the question of morale. When we were successful with Brylcreem and Macleans in the U.S.A. our sales went up everywhere else. Our overseas executives were stirred by our success in the toughest market of all and became 'believers'. Thus I finish where I began, in believing that in the long run the future of Beechams rests on success in the U.S.A.

17 *The End of an Era*

When I became Managing Director, Beechams had no set rules for retirement of Directors, although the Pension Plan was geared to retirement at age 65 for men and 60 for women. Even so, some executives, particularly those with relatively short service and therefore inadequate pensions, were allowed to continue to work past their 65th birthday. Directors were governed by the Companies Act 1948 and every year shareholders were asked to confirm in office those past 70 years of age. During my years as Managing Director we had three, Sir Arthur Marshall, Hubert Meredith, and the Chairman, Lord Dovercourt (previously Sir Stanley Holmes).

On my appointment as Chairman in 1958 I recommended to the Board that we should alter our Articles to provide that all Directors should retire at 70 and this was put to the shareholders and approved. Sir Arthur Marshall had died and we only had Hubert Meredith left. He was very cross with me for ousting him, but I really bore him no ill will. I just felt that it was wrong to allow Directors to continue in office past 70. Indeed, I believed that in general the average age of British executives was too high and I was determined to get it down in Beechams. I was not averse to one or two 'elder statesmen' on the Board but they must not dominate it. So far as the executives were concerned, I believed that very few should be allowed to carry on beyond 65 and that many should retire before that. In my view then, and now, men should ideally reach top executive rank in their 40s. By this I mean the top positions in the various Divisions, including the position of Divisional Chairman. It followed that at age 60 onwards they would have been operating at the top for close on fifteen years and in a company growing at the rate of 10 per cent per annum they would at the end be running a business nearly three times as large.

By 1967–68 Beechams' sales had grown nearly seven times and its profits seven and a half times since 1950–51. During that period, the Retail Price Index increased from 66 to 120, so that after allowing for inflation we had grown roughly three and a half times. The Group was now a different animal and needed a different sort of management. However much I divisionalized and delegated, everyone would expect me to continue to put my finger into every pie and, whether they did or not, I probably would. However, I should inevitably be doing so more and more superficially and this would frustrate a lot of top executives.

It was clear to me that I ought to retire at 65 but I could not decide on a successor at that date. Doug Stafford had already intimated that he wished to take things more easily and retire at 60. There were two obvious future contenders but they were both too young and needed more time in the firing line running their Divisions. I therefore looked outside for someone to take over for a maximum of seven years and in that time to give the two contenders ample opportunity to prove themselves. Again Kenneth Keith came to my rescue by informing me that Sir Ronald Edwards was nearing the end of his contract with the Electricity Council and might be available. I knew Ronnie because of his Business Seminars at the London School of Economics to which I had contributed. He was an accountant, an economist, and an educationalist and – I thought – ideally suited to give Beechams a completely different style from that I had developed. Sir George Bolton had once said to me of a particular individual that he had achieved wonders as a rebel but that he had to know when to 'join the club'. I thought that it was probably time for Beechams to take a less contentious course and that for this purpose it would be helpful to be led for a few years by a member of the Establishment.

Ronnie and I had several talks and he agreed to succeed me but, of course, not before suitable arrangements had been made as to his successor at the Electricity Board. He joined the Beecham Board as a Director on 1 May 1968 and finally took over as Chairman, on 1 November 1968.

This book is an account of Beechams during my term of

office which effectively ended with the financial year 1968–69. In regard to the succeeding years under Sir Ronald's leadership it should be said that the Group has continued to grow and that serious problems have only arisen in that part of the Group where I continued in office for a time. I now believe that I should have given much more thought to retirement from the Chair of Beecham Inc. in the U.S.A. before I did, and that I stayed on there at least a year too long. The Group failed to achieve all my ambitions in a number of areas. I can mention soft drinks, where I wanted to see us established as the most efficient producer throughout the United Kingdom. Then there was the failure to develop our proprietary business in Europe and our troubles in the U.S.A., where my ambitions were very great.

It hurt me to have to leave so many problems to my successor. I personally always aimed high and I suppose my ambitions always exceeded our capacity to perform, but I make no apology for this. High ambitions add spice to life and I personally would prefer to aim for the heights, even if eventually I have to be content with some lower ground. However, in spite of our failures the mythical investor who had put £100 in Beechams in March 1951, and taken up two rights issues, would by March 1969 have had an investment worth £2,553. Whilst I make no claim that this was unique it was not bad going and put a financial measure on the success we had achieved in turning a company regarded in 1951 as a high-risk investment, into one of Britain's 'blue chip' corporations.

However, we were a professional team, all of whom had risen from the ranks. I do not think any of us felt that our first duty was to the shareholders. The company came first and we were intensely proud of Beechams and of what we had made of it. We believed in its destiny and were dedicated to building a great international company capable of competing with the powerful U.S. corporations which dominated so many of the markets in which we were involved. Profits were the measure of our success and the means by which we had to grow. The proportion retained in the business had steadily increased until it exceeded that paid out to shareholders. During the period

April 1951 to March 1971 we paid to the British Government
£78,995,000 in taxes and paid the Ordinary shareholders
£55,032,000 in net dividends, from which they paid further
taxes. In addition, foreign and Commonwealth Governments
took from us taxes totalling approximately £27,722,000. This
left £56,817,000 ploughed back into the business and without
these profits we could not have grown.

In the process of building Beechams we had created much
employment, set a high standard of working conditions
throughout the Group, and had been innovators of many
personnel practices. I have already referred to our non-
contributory pension schemes. In 1957 we added a provision
that employees who left our services for *any* reason other than
misconduct, had all the pension premiums paid by the company
in respect of their employment applied to the purchase of a
paid-up pension at age 65. When I put this to the Board Kenneth Keith remarked that I was 'before my time'. We had
steadily reduced the differences existing in the treatment of
factory and clerical staff until there was complete parity.
There was a substantial death benefit attached to the Pension
Plan, reduced payments were continued to wives on their
husband's deaths, and there were very generous life insurance
benefits. As already mentioned, we had a profit-sharing scheme
which, when I retired, was providing an annual sum approxi-
mating to a little over 10 per cent of annual wages or salaries.
I could continue with this catalogue but I hope I have said
enough to show that we did our best to make everyone feel
that they belonged.

How did all this come about? I suppose different people
would place their emphasis differently but there would not be
a real conflict of opinion amongst those who were there. I
believe that men like Mac, John Rintoul had he lived, and
Doug Stafford, would all in their different ways agree with
most of the views that I am going to express.

Obviously Beechams would not be what it is today without
the penicillin discovery. This more than anything else changed
our character, but in soaking up some of our best executives
it also, in my opinion, damaged our proprietary business for a

few years. Then again we would not have made the discovery without the unique collection of high-quality branded products which supplied us with the profits against which we had to charge the cost of research in the early years. For these we were indebted to Philip Hill, whose prescience led him to acquire them and at the same time the companies on which our overseas development was to be based.

It is interesting to note that in 1968–69 Brylcreem was providing the Group with worldwide net profits of nearly £3 million. The other three brands each yielding profits of £1 million (plus or minus £100,000), were Lucozade, Macleans Tooth Paste, and Eno's. Beecham's Powders and Phensic combined also yielded over £1 million. These were the products that led the way in the first ten years and I have put them in what I conceive to be their order of importance. In the early days nothing can have been more important than Lucozade which was growing so rapidly. For instance, in 1958–59 it contributed profits of £1½ million, much more than any other brand at that date.

It must be remembered that in the period before the last war the advertised products on the market were mostly the survivors of many thousands of products put out by pharmacists and others, originally in their own shops; or they were made by people like A. C. Maclean for supply to chemists, hairdressers, and the like. Lucozade was evolved by W. W. Hunter in his chemist's shop in Newcastle; Eno's was first made up by J. C. Eno, a chemist, also in Newcastle; Macleans Tooth Paste started life as one of many own-name tooth pastes put up under the chemist's own name and address and often carrying their own brand. Brylcreem was first supplied to hairdressers and sales were built in hairdresser shops. Beecham's Powders was the only highly successful pre-war product evolved by Beechams and launched as an advertised proprietary product in the first instance.

All but the last-named product had been tried and tested in the market place before they were advertised and it was abundantly clear that they had great intrinsic merit. The superiority of glucose over sugar has still not been fully accepted by the scientific world, but the public have recognized it in their continued loyalty to Lucozade. The unique Brylcreem formulation still provides the best method of controlling men's hair, and Macleans Tooth Paste really does clean teeth better. Eno's is an extremely safe buffered antacid and Beecham's Powders are probably still the best remedy for colds. Therefore we had the products to hand and what we had to do was to market them efficiently.

We were, I believe, the first British marketing company. I ought to define what I mean by 'marketing' and cannot do better than quote from a paper I presented to one of Sir Ronald Edwards's seminars in 1968:

What is Marketing

The word 'marketing', like so many others, has different meaning for different people. In its widest sense, it describes both a management philosophy and a marketing process which stems from that philosophy.

Marketing executives naturally tend to concentrate on the complex and sophisticated techniques used in the process and to take the philosophy for granted. On the other hand those who have no practical experience of business are liable to look only at one part of the process – for example, advertising – and to ignore the philosophy. Because they do not comprehend the whole, they fail to understand the function of any particular part and this can lead to ill-informed criticism of some of the instruments of marketing.

I think it is important to understand both the philosophy and the process, because I believe that much of the trouble affecting the British economy today stems from a failure in competitive marketing.

The Marketing Concept

The marketing concept is based on two propositions. First that consumer choice is the decisive element in business. Second, that in an age marked by rapid technological change, better education, and higher living standards, the public expects improved products and will buy them when offered in an acceptable form and price range.

Companies must therefore seek out their potential customers, find out what they want, make it to the highest feasible standard, distribute it, and persuade the customers to try it. After that, it is the user's experience of the product that counts. No amount of marketing techniques will bring about a repeat sale to a customer who has decided that a product's performance does not measure up to the claims that were made for it.

It will be clear from this short description that marketing begins and ends with the consumer. It should also be clear that the consumer will only be sovereign if he has the power to take his business elsewhere. If there is no 'elsewhere', that is if there is no effective competition, there can be no consumer sovereignty.

Marketing and Competition

To my mind, the most important thing about marketing is that it is a competitive activity. In fact, marketing can only exist in a competitive economy. If there is insufficient competition, suppliers can consult their own convenience and sell what it suits them to produce. In a competitive economy, the consumer's convenience is paramount and suppliers must address themselves to producing what consumers want to buy. Marketing is therefore a product of effective competition. There is no question of the chicken and the egg here. Competition comes first. If there is no effective competition, there will be no need for marketing.

I think it is vital to establish this point because marketing is becoming an 'in' word and business is now being exhorted to step up its marketing efforts in order to put the British economy on a sounder basis. Those who demand more effective marketing must first press for a more competitive economy.

In my early days neither the Board nor the Chief Executive of most British companies concerned themselves much with 'selling' or with what the customer was saying about their products. Indeed, the Sales Manager was rarely on the Board and he was supposed to go out and sell what top management decided to make. N. F. Fabricius introduced me to 'marketing'. Of course, I had been brought up under A. C. Maclean who was a marketing man by temperament. He believed in 'hunch' and in looking for and exploiting any opportunity that presented itself. But Fab, who had built Brylcreem, used to take and study the Nielsen data. He induced me to follow him and also to take an interest in consumer research, then in its infancy. When I took charge of Beechams, County Laboratories, which was responsible for Brylcreem, Silvikrin Shampoo, Amami, etc., were the most thrustful marketeers and the Beecham Toiletry Division was built on them.

In businesses selling advertised proprietary products, such as Beechams was before the penicillin discovery, everyone in top management should be a 'marketing' man. By this I mean someone who understands the principles of marketing and who thinks and acts in accordance with those principles. If the accountants spend their time seeking to catch out the marketing department, or do not understand enough of marketing to be able to contribute by helping to maintain sound financial principles, then there is chaos. Ideally, the executives in the Marketing Department should also receive a financial and administrative training and the accountants, the administrators, and the technical men should have been through a marketing course. They should then be able to co-operate with knowledge and appreciation of each other's points of view.

I took a close interest in Ashridge Management College, which concentrated on relatively short post-experience courses, and I eventually became Chairman of the Governors. We included a strong financial element in our management courses, ran courses giving financial knowledge for marketing men, and spent a lot of effort in broadening the knowledge of young British executives. In those days the big difference between the British and American executive was the broad theoretical background of the latter. Most young American executives had some business degree or other, which at least gave them some appreciation of finance, accounting, and administration as well as marketing. This was not true of the British executive and the average brand manager could no more than add up.

At one of our Beecham meetings, we had been addressed by our Financial Director, Mike Spry, on some subject. As we walked out, two of our Directors, both marketing men, were together and one said to the other, 'Did you understand what he was talking about?' The other replied, 'Not a word'. One must be fair and say that the accountants made things more complex than necessary but, all the same, very few marketing men could read a set of accounts and they were quite unable to appreciate the financial and administrative effect of multiplying sizes, designing queer shapes or a great variety of shapes, and proposing complex trade terms which were difficult to administer or to monitor. We had to work hard to overcome this ignorance on the one hand, and the complete ignorance of, and lack of sympathy for, marketing on the part of our accountants.

However, nothing works properly without leadership from the top and this means that the Chief Executive must be a marketing man. He may have started life as a chemist, an engineer or an accountant, but he must think and act like a marketing man and understand the principles governing product development, advertising, pricing, and selling.

In the early years I attended the principal advertising meetings relating to our main products. Then when Divisional Management became responsible, I expected the Chairmen of Divisions to do the same. Naturally, everything depends on size, but for the vital products I would never approve of contact with the advertising agent resting solely with brand managers. The latter could sharpen their teeth and prove their worth on the lesser brands. I believe that the Chief Executive has to lead, and I cannot see how he can do so effectively unless he participates in 'marketing'.

Marketing is a very large subject and I must not turn this chapter into a text book. However, perhaps I can illustrate some of the marketing problems that we had to face. First of all, if we were to grow at the rate of 10 per cent per annum in real terms (our planned rate) then we needed to double our size in seven years. Clearly, we should either have to capture a larger and larger share of our existing markets or we should have to invade new ones. I was against adding more and more brands with only small potential and we chose to go for a larger share of existing large markets such as hairdressings, dentifrices, and shampoos, and at the same time to drive into growing large markets such as deodorants, hairsprays (which we did too slowly), and soft drinks. We also went into confectionery and would probably have stayed in and continued our effort to build by acquisition had we not made the antibiotics discovery. Furthermore, we were constantly examining new markets. We looked hard at soaps and detergents, pet foods, and animal supplementary foods. Had it not been for the discovery we should undoubtedly have gone after pet foods; as it was we chose to acquire Vitamins Ltd. with its animal foods and medicines. This enabled us to market some of our antibiotics for animals.

Again, if we were to grow at our planned rate a good deal of this *must* come from overseas. In 1951 Brylcreem had at least 50 per cent of the home hairdressing market, Macleans Tooth Paste nearly 25 per cent of the home dentifrice market, and Beecham's Powders and Phensic together held about 20 per cent of the home analgesic market. Lucozade had no competition to speak of and in shampoos our products held at least 25 per cent of that market. Our drive into the U.S.A. was dictated by these facts plus the need to learn to compete with the great U.S. companies whom we should have to face around the world.

It was also clear that to compete effectively with the Americans we should have to match them in product development and improvement. To meet this need we increased the size of our Toiletry Product Development Laboratories at Brentford and set up a new laboratory at Beecham Inc. in the U.S.A. These are examples of some of our top-level marketing decisions, which were arrived at after discussions at the Chairman's Management Committee held at Beecham House every month.

I do not believe that we could have achieved what we did unless we had possessed some men at the top who were of high calibre. Most of these men joined Beechams with companies which were acquired, but some were with us from the early days and others were engaged as relatively junior executives. One or two came in at high level but certainly all the men who have reached the Beecham Board came up through the ranks. It is also remarkable that Beechams now have so many top executives who started life in one or other of its factories as a chemist or as a manager. No doubt our antibiotics discovery was responsible for this unusual state of affairs. The pharmaceutical business calls for a different kind of marketing animal and Doug Stafford was very shrewd in pulling out chemists like Bob Wilkins, Ronnie Halstead, and Frank Lomax to take on marketing and general management duties. These men had been brought up in a marketing atmosphere and took to marketing pharmaceuticals like ducks to water. They are all now Beecham Group Directors.

We were one of the first British companies to practise marketing in the American style. Indeed, I believe that we improved on American practice by requiring the Chief Executive to lead the marketing team. Our U.S. advertising agency expressed surprise (and pleasure) at the fact that I regularly attended their meetings and that Maurice Bale, our President, both accompanied me and led in my absence. Admittedly this made things difficult for our brand managers but at least they and the agency knew where they stood. The broad overall policy in regard to Brylcreem and Macleans advertising was laid down for them and they were left with the problems of its execution.

It is my firm conviction that none of our main brands would have made the progress that they did without this leadership from the top. I have talked about Lucozade, the translation of Macleans' Danish advertising, the modernization of Eno and its consequences to our worldwide business, and the concentration of Beecham's Powders and Phensic on colds and headaches respectively. These are examples of the many occasions when the top men were able to overcome national or departmental rivalries, or the advertising agents, and insist that success in one place should be exploited elsewhere, that packages should be rationalized and improved, and that formulae should be updated. Finally, the fact that the top men led the marketing teams meant that decisions could be taken quickly both to exploit success and to pull out from failure. This, to my mind, was the crucial test of management.

Writing this book has caused me to look back with considerable joy and nostalgia. I certainly enjoyed my life in the Group and I hope that most of my collaborators did too. We were not an 'establishment' company and had no ambitions to become one. Some little time after I joined the Board of I.C.I. in 1966 one of my colleagues there compared himself and myself to 'barrow boys'. I did not feel very flattered by the comparison but I suppose it is true that during the whole of our period of growth we suffered from the British prejudice against hard selling and heavy advertising. It was, and probably still is, believed that by hard selling and unscrupulous or reckless advertising, one can foist on to the public bad products, or moderate products at unjustified prices. When they joined the Group it was interesting to witness some of the Mortons executives expecting us to teach them how to advertise their run-of-the-mill jams and other grocery items and achieve large sales. They found it difficult to believe that advertising is something that can only be used profitably to sell the highest quality and that everything else can best be sold on price.

We had the high-quality products and 'sold' them. In the process we often crossed swords with the Civil Servants who were, I believe, always prejudiced against, and jealous of, success. I do not regret my aggressive attitude nor do I think that it harmed the company, but I accept the fact that circumstances change and that my outlook was no longer appropriate to the Beechams of 1970. Beechams consists on the one hand of pharmaceuticals and on the other of toiletries, cosmetics, proprietary medicines and the related health drinks and soft drinks. This is not nearly so complex a collection as in Unilever, or in Warner Lambert or American Home Products of the U.S.A., to take only three examples. Furthermore, Beechams has not nearly reached optimum size by comparison with many of its worldwide competitors. Indeed, it has only just become large enough to contemplate splitting pharmaceuticals from the proprietary business worldwide. I see no reason therefore why it should not continue to grow, as it has done so far since I left the scene.

Growth nevertheless brings its own problems, so far solved by very few big British companies and certainly by none of the nationalized industries. How does one assure that sufficient attention is paid to the interests of the mass of the employees? How can their interests be balanced with those of the customers, the shareholders, and the public?

If the mass of the people are to continue to accept the free-enterprise system as we know it today – or as we can modify it – then they must feel an integral part of it. They must feel that they 'belong' and are part of an enterprise that they respect. They must see a secure future in that enterprise and a chance to progress. There is all too much evidence that a great many employees in Britain today have no such feelings and it is surely one of management's most important duties to address itself to this problem.

I hope that Beechams will be in the van of a movement working towards a world when the strike will be regarded as an anachronism, and when the Trade Unions will have changed their character and will no longer be led by men looking backwards – or forward to chaos and Communism – but by those who recognize Unions as part of a structure to achieve social justice and happiness. Above all I hope that they will recognize that happiness and a high standard of living both flow from efficiently operated businesses. I personally do not believe that man can be happy unless he can take pride in his work and feel proud that he is doing a good job. It seems to me that the combination of mass production and Trade Unionism is destroying this sense of pride in one's work and I am convinced that this need not be so.

Beechams has always made efforts to make employees feel that they belong, but I do not believe that in my time we went far enough. I hope that the company will join with others, like Marks & Spencer and I.C.I., to blaze a trail that can be followed and improved on by others and that eventually there will open up a vista that will enable the mass employers to arrive at a solution of their deep problems.

The reader may feel that the last few paragraphs are out of character for a man who has consistently advocated the merits of competition and the pursuit of profit, but I would contest this view. I have never been concerned with short-term objectives. To be successful in the long term it is, in my opinion, necessary to adopt strong principles and to pursue only long-term profits. Nothing infuriates me more than the management that is concerned more with short-term profits than with the company's future health. To cut research or advertising expenditure without good reason; to extract uneconomic prices from suppliers, or cheapen quality to maintain margins; to pursue unethical marketing policies; to fail to foster the interests of the staff or adjust their earnings in the light of market conditions – all these may yield short-term profits but they will harm the company long term. No company can have illustrated more clearly how the pursuit of high principles yields long-term high profits than Marks & Spencer, and to have had the privilege of talking and listening to Lord Sieff was one of my great joys. May Beechams keep pace with this great company and with others pursuing the same path and may they all help to demonstrate that competition and the profit motive, intelligently applied, are still by far the most effective way to achieve a better tomorrow.

Index

Accounts problems, 104–5
Advertising, 34, 79–80
  Brylcreem, 28, 84
  budgets for tooth paste, 9
  increasing budgets, 105
  Maclean's account to Bensons, 10–11
  Macleans Peroxide Tooth Paste, 7
  Macleans Stomach Powder, 12
  on television, 109
Alexander, Bob, 72, 119
Alka-Seltzer, 119
Allen and Hanburys Ltd., 4
Amami, 23, 29, 31, 32, 70
  decreasing profit margin, 40
Ambrose, Bill, 70, 153
American Home Products Corporation, 21
Amery, Rt. Hon. L. C. M. S., 20
Amino-acids, 76, 135
Ampicillin, 51, 168, 184
Ampliclox, 170
Anadin, 81
Analgesics, 80
Andrews Liver Salt, 22, 27
Anti-gas ointment, 37
Armstrong, Frank, 98, 107
Ashton & Parsons, 90
Aspirin, 81
Aspro, 81
Aspro-Nicholas Ltd., 164
Astor, Margaret, A.G., 174
Astra, A.B., 177
Atherton, Bill, 120, 123
Ayerst Laboratories, 184

B.O.A.C. buildings, 102
Bale, Maurice, 119, 125, 130, 154, 155, 180, 184
  transferred to England, 127
Batchelor, Ralph, 146, 163, 165
Bayer, A.G., 169, 177, 179

Bayer Aspirin, 22
Beaverbrook, Lord, 66
Beecham, Sir Joseph, 77
Beecham, Thomas, 77
Beecham (Canada) Ltd., 72, 119, 127
Beecham Estate & Pills Ltd., 77
Beecham Export Corporation Ltd., 36
Beecham Foods Ltd., 101–13
  acquire lease of ex-B.O.A.C. premises, 102–3
  fall in profits, 106
Beecham Group Ltd., 1
  Board in 1949, 65
  discuss possibility of setting up Research Board, 46
  organization chart (1962), 151, 152
  overseas management reorganized, 72
  profits from main companies (1951), 71
  sales by outlet type (1951), 113
Beecham Inc., 180–8
Beecham Maclean Holdings Ltd., 23
Beecham Overseas Ltd., 71
Beecham Products Inc., 127, 128
Beecham Products Ltd., 127
Beecham Research Laboratories Ltd., 17, 45–58, 135
  acquires Brockham Park, 50
  advantages for Group, 53
  budget problems, 72–3
  committee of investigation, 62–3
  principles laid down, 46–7
  proposed method of financing, 53
  reprint of proposals for formation, 52–8
  transferred to Macleans, 63
Beecham's Lung Syrup, 31

Beechams Pills Ltd., 1, 23, 31, 70
  buy Covent Garden, 77
  first sold in Wigan (1842), 77
  formed (1928), 77
  original directors, 78
Beecham's Powders, 70
  advertising claims, 81
  first launched (1926), 77
Bencard, C. L., Ltd., 70, 74, 75, 141,
    145, 177
  merged with Beecham Research
    Laboratories Ltd., 166
Benson, S. H., 10
Bishop, Hazel, Industries, 134
Blend-a-med tooth paste, 173
Blendax A.G., 173
Board meetings, 28
Body Mist, 156, 160
Bonet, F., 178
Bonet, Federico, S. A., 177
Boots Company Ltd., 90
Booz Allen & Hamilton, 173
Bristol, William, 137
Bristol Laboratories Inc., 144
Bristol-Myers Co., 81, 133, 141
Bristow's Lanolin Shampoo, 70, 74
British Drug Houses, 16
Brixner, Karl, 173
Brockham Park, 50
  research laboratory set up, 52, 61-2
Brown, David, 146
Broxil, 167
Brush, Alvin, 184, 185
Brylcreem, 1, 25, 28-9, 70, 84-5, 117
  low profit margin, 40
  profits, 73
  U.S. advertising, 122
  U.S. sales
  war-time production problems, 43-4
Brylfoam, 85
Buckley, Maj.-Gen. J., 60, 117
  leaves Board of Beecham Group, 64-5
  profit participation scheme, 69
  projected appointment as Managing
    Director of Beecham Group, 63, 64
Bufferin, 81

Cadbury Fry, 159
California Syrup of Figs, 22
Canned foods, 111-12
Carbenicillin, 170, 179

Carter, H. W., & Co. Ltd., 98, 156
  merger to form Beecham Foods, 102
Carters Little Liver Pills, 80
Celbenin, 167, 168
Chain, Sir Ernst, 62, 91, 110, 138
  achieves scientific recognition, 165
  moves to Rome, 139
Chance, Michael, 55
Charley, Dr Vernon, 98
Chesebrough-Ponds Ltd., 133
Chloramphenicol, 169
Cicfa Co. Ltd., 31
Cloxacillin, 170
Coca-Cola, 89, 96-8, 157
Colgate-Palmolive Ltd., 21
Colgate Tooth Poste, 8, 9
Conditions of employment, 18
Confectionery, 158-9
Contracts of service, 24
Coombe, Simon, 96
Corona drinks, 156
Coty, 174
County Chemical Co. Ltd., 84
County Laboratories Ltd., 70
  acquire toiletry products from Mac-
    leans, 75
County Perfumery Co. Ltd., 28, 70
  bought by Philip Hill, 25
Covent Garden Properties Co. Ltd.,
    77
Crest, 124
Cripps, Sir Stafford, 94
Culver, Alberto, Co., 134

Davies, J. H., 70, 76, 79, 153
DeFriece, Frank, 181, 182, 187
Dinneford & Co. Ltd., 23, 32, 70, 91
  taken over by Macleans, 43
Dinneford's Magnesia, 32, 83
Directors' retirement age, 189
Disprin, 81
Dole Pineapple, 114
Dorland Advertising Ltd., 107
Dovercourt, Lord, 189
  see also Holmes, Sir Stanley
Dr Cassells Tablets, 31, 90
Dodds, Sir Charles, 45, 47, 56, 135, 139
  Chief Consultant, 62
Doyle, Peter, 146, 163, 165
Drugs, Ltd., 85
Du Lundi, 156, 160

Dunbar, Gordon, 62, 91
  Managing Director of Beecham Export Corporation Ltd., 36

Eagle Star Insurance Co. Ltd., 64
Edwards, Sir Ronald, 1, 164, 187
  takes over as Chairman, 190
Endocrines-Spicer Ltd., 90
Eno, J. C., Ltd., 28, 70, 91
Eno Proprietaries Ltd., 1, 28, 29, 33
  bought by Philip Hill, 25
  purchased (1938), 114
  share price falls, 22
Eno-Scott and Bowne Inc., 71, 116
Eno's 'Fruit Salt', 29, 33, 83, 114
  packaging, 93
  war-time production, 92
  worldwide sales, 28
European operations, 171-9
Export trade, 33-4

Fabricius, N. F., 28, 70, 85, 117
  committee of investigation into research, 62
  died (1960), 151
  problems with Brylcreem, 43-4
Fabricius, Tony, 154, 176
Farmoceutici Italia S.p.A., 177
Farquharson, John, 72, 163
Fenston, Felix, 102
Fermentation plant, 141-4
  erected at Brockham Park, 146
Ferraplex B, 177
Field, Eric, 12
  Fynnon Salt advertising, 18
Fischer & Fischer, 160
Fleming, Sir Alexander, 138
Forhans Tooth Paste, 9
Frisch, Dr H. R., 55
Fynnon Ltd., 16
Fynnon Salt, 14, 15-18, 33, 70, 83
  process patented, 17
  60% of business bought by Macleans, 16

Garden, R., Ltd., 61
Germolene, 31
Gibson, John, 25
Glaxo Laboratories Ltd., 144
Gleem, 124
Glucose shortage, 42

Glycerine, 37-8
Godden, Ted, 176
Goldman Sachs and Co., 182
Graham, S. J., 66
  appointed Personnel Director of Beecham Group, 67
Gregory, Henry, 27, 78
Grocery trade, 59-60, 100-13
  Beecham Group acquires firms, 60-1
  problems of streamlining operations, 74
Groom & Clean, 133
Gwarkin, F. A. S., 22, 51

Halstead, Ronnie, 127, 130, 155, 164, 167, 184, 187
Hart, Ralph, 101
Hart, W. H. & Sons Ltd., 61, 74
Harwoods Laboratories Ltd., 90
Hedley, Thos. & Co. Ltd., 101
Heilbron, Sir Ian, 62, 147, 163
Hewett, F. C., 12
  becomes Sales Director, 20
Hill, Philip, 1, 23, 24, 29, 36, 78
  death (1944), 59
  develops interest in scientific medicine, 45
  initial involvement with Beechams, 77
Hill, Philip, and Partners Ltd., 24
Hill, Wilfred, 84
Hiltone Bleach, 70, 85
Hobrow, Bernard, 23, 25, 27, 47, 60
  committee of investigation into research, 62
  leaves Board of Beecham Group, 64
Holden, R. W., Ltd., 61
Holloways Ointment, 31, 32
Holloways Pills, 31, 32
Holmes, Sir Stanley, 26, 27, 78, 116, 189
  becomes Chairman of Beecham Group, 59
  Board attack, 64
  memorandum on management, 30-5
Hooper, Sir Frederic, 110
Horder, Lord, 15
Horlicks, 62, 80, 160
Horse-chestnuts
  used for boiler fuel, 43
  used to make glucose, 42-3

Houchen, A. E. V., 85, 87
  becomes Chairman of Beecham Food
    and Drink Division Ltd., 153
  becomes Chairman of Beecham Foods
    Ltd., 89
Hunts (Yarmouth) Ltd., 157

Idris Ltd., 157
Imperial Chemical Industries Ltd., 201
Iron Jelloid Co. Ltd., 31, 70
Iron Jelloids, 81
Irving's Yeast-Vite Ltd., 31
  see also Yeast-Vite Ltd.

Jaeger Holdings, Ltd., 40
James, F., 74
James, F. (Newport) Ltd., 59
James, W. D., 110
Jones, Evan, 16

Keith, Kenneth, 64
Kidson, G. H., Ltd., 61
Koch, Ernst, 17, 26, 36, 55–6, 61
  asked to resign from Board of
    Research, 63
Kolynos Tooth Paste, 9

Laboratoires Delagrange, 177
Lactopeptine, 31
Lancaster products, 175
Lane, Philippa, 68
  appointed Personnel Director, 67
Lazell, H. G.
  becomes Secretary of Beechams Pills
    Ltd., 27
  joins Board (1936), 20
  Joint Assistant Managing Director of
    Beechams Group, 61
  Managing Director of Macleans,
    36–7
  offered Managing Directorship of
    Beecham Group, 64
Lloyd, Dr E. L., 85–6, 101
Lomax, Frank, 153, 164, 167, 176, 178
London Press Exchange Ltd., 109
Lucozade, 25–7, 41–2, 70, 74, 83, 96,
    105, 113, 157
  advertising, 80, 107
  made subsidiary of Beecham
    Research Laboratories Ltd., 63
  merger to form Beecham Foods, 102

Mac Brand Antiseptic Throat Sweets,
    70
McGeorge, Walter, 6–7, 61, 139
  appointed Managing Director of
    Beecham Research Laboratories
    Ltd., 51
  Managing Director of Beecham
    Research Laboratories, 56
McGregor, Dr Alexander, 51
McKenna, Reginald, 24
Maclean, Alex, C., 4
  resigns from Board, 20
  sets up Maclean Ltd., 5
Maclean, Ashley, 20
  goes to Canada, 36
Maclean, Guy, 20
Maclean, Professor Hugh, 11
Macleans Ltd., 1, 33, 70
  author becomes Company Accoun-
    tant, 5
  bought by Philip Hill, 25
  factory in danger during war, 36
  Great West Road premises, 15
  management problems, 75
  Park Royal premises, 11
  problems of rationalization, 74
Maclean's Stomach Powder, 7, 11–15,
    33, 70, 83
Macleans Tooth Paste, 7–11, 29, 33,
    70, 74, 154
  expanding range, 185–6
  marketing in U.S.A., 129–32, 133–4
McLure, Don, 83, 155
Management, 161–2
Marchon Products Ltd., 86, 87–8
Marketing, 194–200
Marketing policy, 34–5
Marks & Spencer Ltd., 201, 202
Marriott, Dr, 55
Mars, Ltd., 159
Marshall, Sir Arthur, 78, 189
Massengill, S. E., Co., 160, 181–2
  merged with Beechams (1971), 186
Meade, Major, 8, 9, 19
  converts Debenture, 11
Merck & Co., 144
Meredith, Hubert, 62, 189
Methicillin, 167
Methionine, 135
Miller, Stanley, 182
Milner, Dr F. H., 55

Mint Products Inc., 117
Moore, Ken, 176
Moore, Norman, 10, 80
Mortimer, Arthur, 91
Morton C. & E., Ltd., 60, 71, 74, 111–12
  merger to form Beechams Foods, 102
Mountain, Sir Brian, 98
  retires from Board, 64
Murphy, Bob, 89, 155
Murray, R. S. & Co. Ltd., 158
Murraymints, 158–9
Myers & Co., 20

National Health Service, 60
The Natural Chemicals Co. Ltd., 32, 90
Nayler, John, 146, 163, 165
Newell, Dr Frederick B., 115
Nicholas, Louis, 77, 78, 90
Nielsen, A. C., Co. Ltd., 101
Nielsen Reports, 85–6, 113, 153
Nissim, Joe, 171
Noble Lowndes & Partners, 68
North of England Lard Refiners Ltd., 61
Nunbetta, 59, 74

Orbenin, 170
Owen, W. & Son, 25
'Own-name' products, 5–6

PLJ, 83, 156, 157
Packaging
  conditions of employment, 18
  war-time tooth paste tubes, 39
Parke Davis, 169
Parry, Donald, 59
Pascall, James, Ltd., 89, 156, 159
Pascalls confectionery, 156
Patten, Mark, 70, 91–2
Penbritin, 2, 168, 169, 179
Penicillin, 127, 137–50, 177
  commercial development, 165–70
  early development, 91
  manufacture in Britain investigated, 51
  pastilles used in dental surgery, 51
Penicillinase, 165, 166
Pension schemes, 68
Pepsodent Tooth Paste, 9

Personnel department
  functions, 67–9
  representation on Board, 66–7
Petley, Bill, 106, 163, 164, 186, 187
Pfizer Inc., 144, 169
Pharmaceutical Society, 13
Phensic, 31, 70, 80
  establishing market, 81
Phillips Milk of Magnesia, 22
Phillips Tooth Paste, 9, 22
Phosferine, 81
Phosferine (Ashton & Parsons) Ltd., 32, 70, 90
Phyllosan, 23, 32, 90
Plough, Abe, 118–19
Powers-Samas, 36, 104
Prices held down during war, 40
Prichard & Constance (Manufacturing) Ltd., 32
Proctor and Gamble, 87
Profits
  by brand (1952/1962), 156
  participation scheme, 69
Public issue, 20–1
Pure Lemon Juice Co. Ltd., 156
Purnells Food Products Ltd., 61
Pyopen, 170

Quosh, 100, 113, 156, 157

Ranks, 62
Reckitt & Colman Ltd., 100
Research
  tax treatment of expenditure, 50
  see also Beecham Research Laboratories Ltd.
Ribena, 83, 98–100, 113, 156, 157
  advertising, 107
Rintoul, John, 65–6, 69, 121, 176
  appointed Managing Director of Beecham Foods, 106
  died (1963), 151
  Overseas Department, 71
  Overseas Div., 94
Ritchie, Harold F., 114–16
Ritchie, Harold F., Ltd., 36, 71, 101, 114–15
Rolinson, Dr George, 146, 163, 165
Rose, Ed, 154, 155
  transferred to England, 127
Rowntree Mackintosh Ltd., 159

Royalties, 54
Royds, George, 28–9, 79–80
  advertising account for Brylcreem, 84

Sainsbury Committee, 170
St Helens, 77
St Joseph's Aspirin for Children, 118
Sampling, 130
Schon, Frank, 87, 88
Schroeder, Helmut, 173
Schroeder, Juergen, 174
Schwartz, Fred, 144, 149
Schweppes, 110
Scientists, 39
  payment of royalties, 54
  rates of pay, 49
  recruitment, 163
  use of outside consultants, 49
Score, 133
Scott & Bourne Inc., 115–17
Scott & Turner Ltd., 27
Scott, Austin, 78
Scott's Emulsion, 114
Scrymgeour, C. T., 78
Share issue, 22
Sherley, A. F. & Co. Ltd., 31, 32–3
Silvikrin, 70, 85, 86, 154
  launched in U.S.A., 125
Smartt, Jack, 68, 109, 153
Social facilities, 19
Sodium sulphate, 16–17
Spahlinger, Henry, 45–7
Spirella Co. of Great Britain Ltd., 5
Sporting facilities, 19
Spry, Mike, 71, 74, 97, 104
Staff
  part-time during war, 41
Stafford, Douglas
  Managing Director of Beecham Research Laboratories Ltd., 70, 74, 75, 89, 127, 153, 166, 176
  joins Group, 91
Sterling Drug Inc., 21, 22, 27
Sullivan, Jim, 98, 109, 111, 113, 153, 155, 164

Tablet making, 41
Tartaric acid, 139
Taxation
  of company executives, 18

Taylors (Cash Chemists) Ltd., 90
Television commercials, 109, 158
  for Brylcreem in U.S.A., 122–3
Tetracycline, 169
Thermogene, 33, 81
Thomas & Evans Ltd., 69, 110–11, 156
Thompson, J. Walter, Co. Ltd., 80
Timmins, A. F. Ltd., 61
Tod, John and James, & Sons Ltd., 61, 74
Townley, Updike & Carter, 115
Truefitt, Charles, 158

U.S. Vitamin Corporation, 181
United States of America
  competition, 48
  operations, 180–8
Updike, Stuart, 126

Veno Drug Co. Ltd., 27, 31, 70, 78, 90
Veno's Lightning Cough Cure, 31
Verburgh, B., 177
Vitalis, 132–3
Voseman Ltd., 156
Vosene Medicated Shampoo, 88–9, 156, 157

Warner Lambert Co., 200
Watney Mann Ltd., 96
Welfare, 66
West, Colin, 184, 185
Whites, Timothy, Ltd., 90
Wigglesworths Peroxide Tooth Paste, 7
Wilkins, Bob
  Assistant Managing Director of Beecham Research Laboratories Ltd., 127, 153, 164, 167, 187
Williams, Henry & Sons Pty. Ltd., 74
Wolseley Fruit Canning Co. (Pty) Ltd., 74
Wood, Craig, 101–2, 103, 104, 105
  resigns, 106
Woolworth, F. W., & Co. Ltd., 5, 8
World War II, 36–58
Wurz, Georges, 175
Wurz, Jean-Pierre, 175

Yeast-Vite, 23, 31, 83
Yeast-Vite Ltd., 70, 78, 90
  see also Irving's Yeast-Vite Ltd.

Zam-Buk, 6